Rocky

The True Story of a Dog Who Adopted Humans Nobody Else Wanted

Snjezana Marinkovic

Copyright ©2024 Snjezana Marinkovic

All rights reserved. No portion of this book may be reproduced in any form without permission from the publisher, except as permitted by U.S. copyright law.

Believe in Love as Love believes in you

CONTENTS

Acknowledgments	vii
Prologue	1
1. Meet Our Little, Untraditional Family	9
2. Divorce	12
3. A Little About Rocky . . .	16
4. Grandma	20
5. Here Comes Zorel	26
6. Dream Child	29
7. Beach	33
8. Hurricane	36
9. Illness	38
10. Accident	42
11. Homeless	45
12. Pandemic	48
13. They Tried to Divide Us	52
14. And The Story Continues	55
15. How About Your Story?	58
16. Working Beside Rocky	65
17. Resemblance Between Dog and His Person is More Than Physical	72
18. Listen To Your Dog; I Wish I Did (More Often)	78
19. Hope	84
20. Bond	98
21. Faith	101
22. I Didn't Let Him Go, I Set Him Free	107
Fly	110
23. Energy Around Us	112
Today I Was In A Hurry	119
I Know You Know	121
24. Reiki	123
25. Animal Communication	134

26. Afterlife	140
Bond	151
27. Letters	152
28. Sign	174
29. Comfort	187
30. Past Life Regression	193
31. Gift	196
Author's Note	229

ACKNOWLEDGMENTS

Special thanks to my editor Jennia D' Lima who went above and beyond to help me with this book.

Joyce Booker and Robert Harrison, thank you for giving the final touch to my work.

Amu Casto thank you for taking beautiful photos of Rocky.

Tina Proffit, Karen Anderson, Kathleen Prasad, Gail Graham, and Brandon Wainwright thank you for your inspiring books.

Thank you, my grandmother, Zora Kostic, for being my guardian angel, and my daughter, Zorel Kostic, for inspiring me to live and write after the biggest tragedy in my life.

And I am forever grateful to you Rocky for adopting me and my child and loving us unconditionally.

PROLOGUE

"Do you have someone you can call?"

A man in scrubs stands before me, waiting for my answer. Just over his shoulder, I can see the emergency room door slightly ajar. Inside, the love of my life is struggling to breathe through an oxygen mask. I want to hope, but I feel that this might be where our story ends. This morning, I have to make a decision—alone, just like I have many times before—but this time is the hardest. What should I do? What should I say? Who could possibly understand that the life I am responsible for is not an ordinary life, and the love pulsing through me is not an ordinary love? My aching heart may wish to call someone, but there is no one to call. There are only two hearts, irrevocably connected, for better or worse, and that has always been more than enough. This love is everything.

I'm not the first to lose someone more precious to me than life itself or, in these last moments, to bargain with God and the universe to let a loved one, to let him, stay. I need him. We need more time together; this cannot be the end.

I study the man's face to distract myself from this harsh reality. His eyes are growing heavy with boredom and impatience. I take a few seconds to find the right words as he glances at the exit door that leads to his personal life and family. I don't expect him to understand that my child and I are about to lose our only family. We have built our lives around Rocky. There's nobody for us to return home to, nobody else to love us.

"Do you have someone you can call?"

The vet's voice echoes in my ears. He turns away and closes the door. I no longer hear my boy's labored breathing, but I know he's still alive, waiting for me to take him in my arms, put him in his favorite spot in the car, and drive him home for our last ride together. Even with these thick walls between us and the cacophony of hospital noise confusing my thoughts, I can feel the softness of his kind soul radiating to me. Even though we are physically apart, I feel his comforting presence. I hear his barking, which has followed me everywhere for twelve-and-a-half years. Now, as always, he waits for me. He's ready to put this cold, sad place behind him, behind us. He won't miss this last ride with me, not my Rocky.

The best love stories are often the most tragic. Losing a loved one is tragic, but is it possible to lose love like it's something as mundane as your keys or phone? Probably, if we think of our beloved as one of our possessions. Does a true love story have an ending? It does if love is nothing but a word within a story. If you are lucky, you've already found someone who opened the door leading you into the story of love where no words are needed. Once you have, you will never look at the world the same way again because you will not speak about that love. You will breathe it in and out like the air around you. Only then will you feel all the happiness carried in other people's hearts as if it were your own, embrace pain like you embrace love, and hold the hopes and dreams of others with care. They, too, will be a part of you.

Even the best romantic love stories can't compare to the epic love story that begins when a dog chooses a human. When he makes his choice, he's on a mission to connect heart-to-heart, soul-to-soul. It may take him some time to build that connection because his person may be swamped in self-doubt and self-criticism. His person may constantly be in a hurry, rushing through life, closing one door after another, turning her head away from others and her back on love. But the dog doesn't give up easily. He works hard until his human is ready to step out of her comfort zone to let him teach her what he teaches best: that forgiving everything you can gives you more time to love everyone you should love.

The dog innately knows the human he is about to teach keeps falling back into old habits. When introduced to something new, it takes the dog days to decompress, weeks to understand it, and months to learn it. Yet he is the simplest being to please. Knowing how complex his human is, his patient nature gives them years to get from judgment to compassion, taking to giving, dividing to uniting, and from barely surviving to living joyfully.

It's not coincidental that one specific dog, who lived in a tight corner, bumped into one specific person and fell irrevocably in love with her. He recognized they were both longing to fit in and that they both longed for unconditional love and security. He assumed that his wagging tail would become a magic wand for this person, and he was one hundred percent right.

He was about to show her that he didn't care about her body measurements, the price tags on her clothes, or the size of her house. He wanted her to know that he only cared about what was inside of her: her true self. He accepted her the way she was even when she didn't. Even when she wasn't aware of the substance of her own being.

Many years passed before she realized what blessings that beautiful dog with different-colored eyes and wolfy coat brought into her life. Many years passed before she understood that the dog's purpose was not to follow her around. Instead, he came to show her that every second is a precious moment that doesn't repeat itself. She could get the best of life if she allowed herself to enjoy it and admitted how lucky she was to find someone to share these beautiful moments of joy with.

But one day, she could no longer see her dog by her side. She could only see people like her who spent most of their time figuring out how to live a long, happy life rather than making someone else feel loved and happy.

Her dog was the exact opposite. For him, she was the entire world, his whole life. He found happiness wherever she was. So his connection to her continued after his beautiful soul—his moment in time—left one realm and entered another.

Rocky showed her the true meaning of that connection, especially after her daughter was born. He was there for all the nursery rhymes, first solid foods, first steps, first games, and first school years. He never strayed far from the crib, stroller, or playground. As a therapy dog who worked with children in her daughter's school, he often peeked inside her classroom to ensure she was doing well.

He adopted two humans, determined to love and care for them, and he did just that. Rocky gave everything, including his own life, to protect two little vulnerable souls roaming around a big, wide world.

Rocky knew they had nobody else but him. He knew how much they needed him . . . his protection . . . his guidance. His floppy ears and lolling tongue invited them to forget about everything wrong in life and have some fun. He understood them like nobody else because he knew how it felt to sit in a corner waiting for his hero—his rescuer—and be overlooked day after day. He knew how it felt when people passed by, paying no attention to his plea for help. He wanted his big and little girls to forget about those who didn't care and to be happy with those who did. Like he was.

With Rocky, his human learned that a wagging tail was an open heart that loved and was always ready to love more, while a human's quickly uttered "I love you" was open to speculation. There was nothing she looked forward to more than feeling a shiny, wet nose landing on her skin as soon as she returned home. His welcome could restore the energy people had drained. It made her feel cherished, beautiful, and worthy of love and kindness. She never slept more peacefully than when his four soft paws and her child's two little hands were beside her. At no time did she love her life more than in moments like those. Yes, she and her daughter once had a wonderful family, and that family was Rocky.

Grief experts suggest talking to your family and friends when you deal with a loss of a loved one. But when a dog is your only family and friend, you have to go beyond people and this world; you have to reach higher. To do that, you must do what your dog has taught you. You must be your own source of consolation. To get to that level, you must first admit, with every piece of your broken heart, that some people do not believe you should grieve when a pet dies.

You can still share what is in your heart. You can show we all have a source of comfort that goes beyond our comfort zone. It's hard to believe, but our wounds begin to heal when we hurt the most. When we allow pain to reach its pinnacle, we can control its intensity. By sharing this with someone—anyone—you may help yourself; you may help others. I'm doing that right now, and I want to cry and smile with you. I want to tell you how one beautiful soul changed my life forever.

This story is about Rocky's love, devotion, and ultimate sacrifice. It is about my experience with love—my experience with such a precious love—and the most valuable experience I could ever have. It is based on lessons he shared with my daughter and me while asking for nothing in return; lessons that transformed two sad, scared, and untrusting hearts. Rocky wanted *us,* his people, to find happiness no matter how impossible that seemed. He didn't

want us to limit our faith to what our eyes could see. He showed us how and why we should believe in the everlasting energy of love. I —*we*—thank him every day for that.

Do you have someone to call when the love of your life is no longer around? Do you have someone who will care? Do you have someone who will understand inexplicably what your heart is going through without saying a word? Someone who will make everything better? If you think you don't, think again. And read the story of Rocky's family—*our* family. Our story is a story of love, and there's always someone to call in such a story. If you matter to them and they matter to you, your call will never go unanswered. Simply call their name and wait. The call is connecting. You are on one end, and they are on the other. Say something . . . anything . . . they are right there. They are listening. You are both ready for a new beginning and ready to feel the embrace of love.

Chapter One
MEET OUR LITTLE, UNTRADITIONAL FAMILY
A Little About Me...

No matter when a journey ends, there is always a path called love. On that path, all is possible. Nothing is divided. All is yours.

I once watched a video showing an alligator trying to break a tiny turtle with his eighty sharp teeth without success. Like that turtle, I survived what the world threw at me as long as I stayed hidden in my shell. I felt lonely but safe while tucked inside my shell. Now and then, I would peek at the sun and allow my heart to feel its warmth, but that was about it. I knew no other way of life. I had no desire to search for a different one. I believed I would spend the rest of my days precisely like that—concealed from the view of others, never needed by anyone, and never, ever unconditionally loved.

Then a puppy arrived. I peeked out from my shell . . . once, twice, and a third time. Then again, and once more just for good measure. I thought, *How come someone has been showing interest in this strange person called* me *for so long? How come he's still there—in the same spot, waiting?* But I could never imagine that he would keep inching closer, trying to fit inside my shell to be with me.

At first, I pushed him out. I wanted to show him that a little puppy needed some fun; he didn't need to hide from the world and waste time with me. A puppy needed more joy and excitement than I could give. A puppy needed someone better than me. Yet he was determined not to leave. There was not a single doubt about that. He was persistent. He made it clear that he had come to stay. He was home.

When I stayed in my shell, he was there with me. On the occasions when I came out of my shell, he was ready to explore the world and share his every little excitement with me. He spent each day waiting for my next move and broke my armor down piece by piece. I talked more, smiled more, and even trusted more. I noticed that the world was full of colors instead of black and white. I felt a warm embrace of love. Love had invited me to dance with life. I took one step, and another, and another. Soon, the armor fell away. With Rocky by my side, I could do anything. In my mind, there was a beautiful, never-ending story. Then, abruptly, everything was back to "normal." Darkness prevailed. Rocky was no longer there.

I built a more robust shell and disappeared under it when Rocky became a spirit. I rarely looked at the sun. Eventually, I stopped seeking the light. I waited for the night and the stars to appear, wondering which one was my Rockstar. I'd never felt so alone and so broken. I felt as though my arms and legs had been amputated. I had to start a new chapter of my life. But how? I didn't want a new chapter to begin. Ever. It was hard to be inside my shell without seeing my puppy's happy face and witnessing his determination to squeeze in just to be next to me. I believed he was the first and would be the last to do that. He was the first and only one to show support and love to my child and me. I needed to endlessly cry and scream in pain, but I also needed to help my daughter with her grief. I needed to keep living.

This is my story. Yours is different, and that is the beautiful thing about existence. We all experience love in different ways. We all grieve in different ways. I can only tell you that no matter how hard it might be for you to believe, there are humans who are shaped more by a dog or another animal companion—I prefer to call them our true soulmates—than people. Those humans who have experienced such love have a void in their hearts after their loss, and sometimes that's a void no one else can fill. You may be one of those humans. Maybe not. Or perhaps you haven't found your true soulmate yet. I did when I found Rocky, and I'll see him again. I'll keep finding him. I'll keep loving him. The world around me ceases to exist when his floppy ears, long sticking-out tongue, and sky-sparkling eyes appear in front of me. He runs toward me. Nowhere else. I want to believe I found him, but he found me. I want to believe my heart is already full of love, but he is still showing me how to love deeper and how to love more.

Chapter Two
DIVORCE

The key to helping a dog is to help yourself.

"We need to take the dog to the shelter. We can get another one when we buy a house." My then-husband wasn't thrilled I adopted a dog while he was away from home.

"He whines all night long," he continued, shaking his head. "I can't sleep."

"He doesn't like to be in his crate." I tried to convince him we needed to give the puppy some time to adjust. "Please give him a chance," I begged.

I was not looking forward to waking up every morning before sunrise to take this energetic, not-yet potty-trained puppy for a walk, but I liked the dog. I liked him so much, and I needed a friend. For days, my then-husband was determined that we must take the puppy back to the dog rescue group that he had been adopted from. I disagreed but nodded without looking at him. Then finally one day, I knew I needed to come up with something better; I needed to say something that would change his mind. I turned toward Rocky, sitting by the front door, and met his eyes. The sadness he carried in them was painful and profound. "Those eyes," I said to my then-husband, "just look at them." I grabbed a bag and started collecting dog toys without saying anything more. He glanced at the puppy and then at me but didn't say a word.

We drove in silence with Rocky sitting in the front passenger seat on my lap. He drooled from stress, and I cried from sorrow. Holding him so close was painful because this was it. We were at the beginning of our life together only moments ago, and now we would soon be going our separate ways. I wanted to believe that such an outcome was better for both of us.

I wiped the drool from Rocky's face, my thoughts racing in every direction. "Fewer responsibilities for me and less anxiety for you. You'll find a good home—a happy home. It's better this way." He lifted his head and gave me a look that said "You can lie to your heart but not the heart of a dog. Dogs are true to you and themselves. Why can't you people do the same? Why can't you fight for me? Why?"

"Look at his begging puppy eyes," I cried.

"I guess . . ." My then-husband sighed. "I guess we . . ." He sighed again. "I'm not sure."

"We should keep him," I insisted, my eyes fixed on Rocky. "Please."

"Okay then," he murmured.

"Yes!" I shouted over and over, louder each time. I buried my hands in Rocky's soft fur and kissed his silky ears. "You're so beautiful," I whispered to him.

On that day, Rocky officially became a member of our household and my child. His new family included an eighty-three-year-old great-grandmother who had recently moved from a nursing home in the Czech Republic to our apartment in Texas. He had to help her adjust to a new environment while he was adjusting himself, which included going to an animal hospital and working with me six days a week. I'm not sure which of these dog duties he was more excited about.

My then-husband was a long-haul truck driver, so we would see him, on average, once a week. Sometimes he only had a few hours to spend with us, and sometimes one whole day before he headed out again. But even that was enough time for him to become attached to Rocky.

He was a good fur-child dad, but he used his "manly force" when things didn't work according to his plans. Luckily, I was the only one in the house who was the target of his rage, including the mental abuse and physical torture. But I was skilled at finding a rat hole, taking my pain with me, and hiding there. Still, this left a mark on Rocky's puppyhood. During those episodes, he was quiet, with his ears down and his tail tucked between his hind legs. He wanted to protect me, but he was too little and too sweet to act on it. Despite his own fear, he stayed close to me, helping my wounds heal and my tears dry. His eyes never lacked care or compassion. With Rocky, for the first time, I saw two reflections: one showed a woman in chains and another showed a woman smiling. Right then, I knew I had to make a choice, so I chose to live.

One and a half years later, I was divorcing my then-husband and learning to breathe again. Grandma, Rocky, and I moved out. Rocky stopped drooling, I stopped crying, and Grandma adjusted to Texas-style heat. It was a good time for a new beginning.

Chapter Three
A LITTLE ABOUT ROCKY...

People will point at your mistakes. Some will inspire you to err more; for dogs, you are just right, perfect just the way you are.

I could never understand how and why Rocky loved people so much. I may be selfish or too cautious, or maybe forgiveness is one of my weakest qualities. Perhaps all of that, but I often couldn't believe my eyes. People sometimes turned their backs on him or pushed him away in dog parks when he stood in front of them waiting to be petted. One minute. Two minutes. Three minutes. Rocky could stay there forever because he was patient, persistent, and needy for love.

Sometimes people threatened both of us when we walked past them. They didn't want us near them or in their neighborhood because we scared their kids or dogs. Maybe because they didn't know us. Perhaps because neither of us had a purebred appearance. No matter their reasons, their stink-eye stares made me sad and uncomfortable, but Rocky just wagged his tail. He tried so hard to show them that it is a beautiful and pure heart that counts. Rocky was determined to show them that when you observe the world around you with understanding and compassion, the world inside of you knows peace and joy. I didn't realize then that he was also teaching me and helping me realize I should always give more than I got. I should always give better.

But luckily, Rocky and I came across many people who loved—or at least liked—dogs. Many of them were drawn to his unique two-colored eyes. Some of them loved the softness of his fur. Others were charmed by the happiness he spread with his form of greeting new friends, which started with helicopter-style tail wagging, followed by quick butt sniffing, then impressive, fast digging, and ended with him rolling in the grass with a huge smile. But no matter what Rocky did, his gentle gaze always settled on me and made my heart flutter. No matter how eager he was to be around other people, that full-body wag he shared only with me was truly something special.

Many people who were uncertain about his wolf-like appearance soon found out that he was a friendly and lovable pup. People who spent even a short time in Rocky's presence found it impossible to feel sad. Even my grandmother, a survivor of two wars and domestic violence, with her severe post-traumatic stress symptoms and a lack of desire for living, smiled when he was next to her. When Rocky was around, there was never a shortage of sniffing, licking, and trying to get his cuteness rewarded with a snack from the plate you were eating from.

Rocky knew how to turn insecurity into confidence and fear into love. His mission in life was not only to show me how to focus on the positive side of everything but also to protect me from myself and others. He knew I was a total wreck and that something had to change so I could repair my life and find a new, healthier path. I had gotten used to staying away from big, merry crowds and living in my deep darkness, and I realized Rocky had become a beacon of light for me. The energy he filled my heart and home with was something I had never experienced.

Now, Rocky makes sure this experience repeats itself each time I think about him and each time my daughter plays with his favorite toy. He also makes sure I enjoy life one moment at a time and show gratitude for everything I have and everything I am right now. I will always be the mom of a curly-haired girl and a furry boy. I am and always will be a human who strives to better herself. I am and always will be someone who knows my heart can be open to everyone or not open at all. Now I know there are no shortcuts to love. Either you take the road and follow the signs life puts in your path or you lose your way. The first sign is often the hardest to understand, but it is the most valuable one. It reads *Love Yourself*.

Now I know why so much suffering existed in and around me. I lived my life with my head buried in the past, taking quick breaks to dream about an unguaranteed future. I was alive but unaware of my breathing. I couldn't go on like that for much longer. I was letting my life slip through my fingers like grains of sand. I didn't know any of that, but the universe did. That's why it sent me Rocky. The higher realms knew very well that I needed to find love and hope, and despite all my disappointments and brokenness, I needed to dig deep inside my heart and find the flickering flame called belief. I needed to learn how to have faith in the good. I needed to know that I could always do more and be better when guided by my dog's beautiful, never judging soul. My Rocky. My always kind and always loving Rocky.

Stars have fascinated me my entire life. I never told a soul about this before. I wasn't open to the wonders that life had to offer. I tried to stick to the five senses that took me places but never where I wanted to stay, never where I truly fit. Still, I wanted to experience and feel the stars beyond those senses. When my grandmother bought me little golden star earrings for my seventh or eighth birthday, every time I wore them, I would secretly check every hour to see whether they were still there.

But when Rocky officially became my dog, I never thought much about his full name—Rocky Rockstar. Months after he left the Earth, guided by his life philosophy—*live in the moment, do what you love*—I started learning about stars and found information on the brightest one in the sky. It is called Sirius or the Dog Star. My first thought was that my Rockstar had returned to the stars where he belonged and where he would shine on me. But I believed and hoped that was only for a while because his heart was still on this rocky planet and in my rocky life.

Chapter Four
GRANDMA

Dogs understand, more than you think.

Even when you leave a toxic relationship, you struggle to discover where you fit into your life's new chapter. At least, I did. Between working three jobs, going to school full-time, and completing classes toward my master's degree, I tried my best to care for Grandma and Rocky. My grandma was bedridden by then and couldn't do much independently. She and Rocky spent most of their time together, bonding and relying on each other. I was fortunate that two of my jobs were close to where we lived, allowing me to come home and check on them during the day.

I often visited them on my lunch break. Once I walked through the front door, I would check if Grandma needed a diaper change. Then I would fix some quick snacks for the two of us and give my boy a couple of his favorite treats. After that, Rocky and I would go for a short walk and, if time permitted, take a power nap together.

I loved those naps. Sometimes Rocky was my soft pillow. Other times, we just snuggled. His breath felt warm on my skin. His paws close to my hands made me feel so peaceful and loved. The only downside of those naps was Rocky's gas-passing habit that tended to wake me again and again, and then I'd oversleep from time to time and be late for work.

My grandmother slept most of the time, and when she didn't, she thought about the past. She spoke very little, and when she did speak, her main topic was people who'd passed on a long time ago. Sometimes she would tell me their names and how much they meant to her. Sometimes she would share a story or two with me. Each of those stories took place in her birth city of Sarajevo, where she spent seven decades of her life.

Grandma was only fourteen years old when World War II took place. Soon after it began, her father and two of her brothers were killed. I believe that instilled a fear in her that everyone she loved would die before their time, but it wasn't until she married my grandfather that she became very fearful, lonely, and angry. Maybe her anger came from being unforgiving toward the man who betrayed her trust and abused her physically and emotionally.

I think I inherited my grandmother's luck in living for years in a dysfunctional marriage. I also inherited the anger, often catching myself looking for a reason for minor arguments that led to enormous explosions. Grandma was unhappy with many unfortunate circumstances unfolding in her life. I was the same. When we had no one else to point our finger at and blame, we were angry at each other, as if afraid to break the cycle of unhealthy emotions.

A victim's state of mind is like a contagious disease that can affect many generations. It releases a lot of destructive energy, continuing to do so until it is transformed. Then a person either realizes that no one is immune from the pain and no one is perfect or continues to focus on what others have done to them and asks, "Why me, God?" In her book *You Can Heal Your Life*, author Louise Hay suggested that as we delve deeper into our traumatic experiences, we may find that we are all victims of victims.

But Grandma's sadness and anger ended on July 10, 2012.

Rocky was with me when I watched her take her last breath. He was with me when the ambulance came and took her away. Rocky spent many days walking around the apartment looking for her. He settled in her room, waiting for her return. The hope in his eyes warmed my heart. Some days, it even made me cry less, though the devastation I felt was still overwhelming. The pain reverberated through every piece of my being, but I wasn't alone. I had Rocky. He supported me every step of the way; he grieved right along with me.

To avoid a space filled with nothing but memories that I wasn't ready to face, we strove to spend most of our time outdoors. We spent countless days and nights walking without a destination in mind and without any interest in our surroundings. I couldn't bear being in that apartment. Every wall, every item, and even every smell reminded me that I had lost the only person who had ever loved me, the only person who took me as a little child into her arms and under her roof. There was nobody else, nobody like my grandmother.

Without Grandma, I could only rely on my own two legs to take me away from my painful thoughts. That didn't help, but my companion did. If I didn't have Rocky next to me, I probably would have given up on life. I wanted to—more than anything else. My boy knew that, so he didn't move from me; he never left my side. He knew that from my first steps in life, I was raised by my grandmother. He knew because he was there. He was part of that family, my family, right from the beginning—but more about that in the following chapters.

Everywhere I turned I felt a warm embrace of the spirit world following my grandmother's transition. My grandmother tried to show me she was well. In my encounters with her soul, orbs of light manifested. Those I saw in my dreams were colorful and of unexplainable beauty. The ones in my home often turned off without me touching a light switch. I describe these experiences more in my book *My Dawn*, published seven months after Grandma's passing.

In one of those beautiful encounters, my grandmother shared that spirits are the first to meet family members yet to be born. She learned that I was a soon-to-be mother to a girl who would have her name. I admit that I was very skeptical about that, and I believed my grandmother was only saying it to make me feel better—nothing new or unusual. She tried to soothe my pain from the other side, just as she did in life. She always worried about me. But as a single woman with no intention of entering a relationship and no desire for motherhood, I didn't know how to process this experience other than to respect the wisdom beyond the physical world surrounding me. And boy, I did that with devotion, passion, and awe.

Not until many years later, when Rocky joined my grandmother, did I start learning about communication with the spirit world. I hadn't been aware that the afterlife is real, and everything that comes from it and those who loved us has something and everything to do with the truth. They learn and grow on the other side as we learn and grow here. We know and grow more when we believe in them as they believe in us.

My grieving heart didn't allow all of my grandmother's messages to come through. Even so, her spirit kept trying. Four years later, while my daughter Zorel and I were visiting Sarajevo and the apartment where my grandmother used to live, I felt her presence again. Zorel and I were sleeping in Grandmother's room when the radio started playing by itself. I was surprised but thought little of it, so I got up, turned it off, and went back to sleep. Soon I was awake again, but this time, I felt a warm kiss on my cheek. That kiss brought a smile to my lips and a tear to my eye. "I love you, Grandma," I whispered.

My grandmother proved she was still watching over me. When a friend "accidentally" took money from my home, my grandmother came into one of her dreams and confronted her. As my friend explained it, she was standing before her and examining her face without saying a word, which made her feel uneasy. "I felt like I had done something I shouldn't," she said. "I'm sorry." As you can assume, the money was eventually recovered, but trust was lost for good.

Months later, when I started dating someone who didn't have good intentions, my grandmother ensured that no appliance in my home functioned properly when that person was around. Whenever we were together, I had that gut feeling that something was not right. One that I, unfortunately, decided to ignore.

Little did I know that I would remember and especially appreciate my grandmother's efforts to communicate with me from the other side many years later. During the most challenging time of my life, they would remind me that, like my grandmother, Rocky never left me. To this day, they both encourage me to wake up smiling in the morning and to be thankful for my daughter, them, us, our family, and the love that truly never dies.

My grandmother often reminded me that she was very well aware of how much she meant to me. On many occasions with my eyes closed, I could see her face and smile and feel her gentle touch. She also tried to show me that the most important human in my life was yet to be born. She did that by sending some beautiful people my way. One of them was a woman called Auntie Mila.

I met this lovely, soft-spoken lady right after I buried my grandmother. Auntie Mila's daughter was buried about thirty feet from my grandmother, and I could see her and her husband every day while I was sitting in front of my grandmother's headstone. One day Auntie Mila approached me and asked me who I had there. "My grandmother," I told her with a sigh.

In the days to come, I learned what a mother feels when her child leaves the Earth long before her time and that a mother's heart never heals from such a loss. I saw how it looks when eyes no longer have light in them.

Auntie Mila gifted me something I would always cherish, not only because it was beautiful, but because it was a clear sign of my grandmother's presence. It was a handmade tablecloth with "Zora" written on it. She said, "A person with that name was once part of my life." I smiled through my tears and mouthed "Thank you."

Chapter Five
HERE COMES ZOREL

It takes a village to raise a child, but only one dog to make that child compassionate, wise, and happy.

Have you ever witnessed how much determination a dog and his little, two-legged child friend have when chasing a ball? They use all their strength to do so, yet they do it naturally and faithfully. They pursue it as if it is one of the earthly wonders rather than a simple rolling object. They enjoy themselves, every bit, every moment.

What do a dog and a child have in common to make them such a dynamic duo? Everything and all. For them, there are no dreams from the past or plans for the future; they are living their dream in the present moment. They are one with their imagination. For them, there is no such thing as making a living. They are just living, content with what they have, and reaching for the stars no matter how small they are.

But one day, they will be separated. Their time will come to say goodbye, but neither will be ready to do so. Whatever they do, time will not be on their side. But is that the end? Or is that when their search for one another begins? Like dawn that's not ready to turn away from a star; like a mountain reaching for a river; like a flower praying to grow its petals up to the tree. Like Rocky and his Zorel, aka the girl with a curl.

Some of the cutest moments were when Rocky, full of pride, started bringing his little sister to the dog park. He always sported the biggest smile while showing her around and introducing her to his friends. *Woof, woof. This is Max. This is my sister Zorel. Woof, woof, this is Jack. My sister Zorel. Woof, woof. Mona. Woof, woof. Zorel.* But Rocky would come between them every time any of the dogs tried to move too close to her and give her one sniff. That was his way of saying "Buddy, you're cool, but please take a step back."

This is what the attention I longed for as a child must look like, I thought while watching Rocky make sure Zorel was never out of his sight and reach. I knew he would be my best teacher in the whole wide world. I was ready to learn whatever he wanted me to learn. Zorel was ready too. She was prepared to follow her only brother everywhere and ready to show him all the fun games she wanted him to play with her.

They always had a new story to share with me when they interacted. Anybody who has ever loved a dog, child, or both would never want to miss any of those stories. Those two taught me all I needed to know about my own life. Their stories were unique and had two sides. One side came from a child who needed a friend, and the other from the dog who became that friend. He walked beside her all his life. He continues to do so through her dreams, wishes, words, and actions.

Rocky spoke to her young soul as no one else did. She saw everything she wished for in life when she looked at him: A mom who is always eager to listen and play with her. A father who drops her off and picks her up from school. A sister who shares her toys with her. A brother who keeps bullies away. A grandma who likes to go on long walks, and a grandpa who makes funny faces when he (accidentally) passes gas. No, my daughter was not growing up in a huge extended family, but she had Rocky to make up for all those play dates with cousins, holiday gatherings, and big birthday parties she never experienced. He was there when she tried her first solid food. He was there when she took her first steps. He was there when she said her first words. He was there when nobody else was willing to listen and play. I didn't want her childhood to resemble mine. I tried to make her happy every day, but I didn't know how. But, like her, I had Rocky to show me what good parenthood should look like. Yes, sometimes it takes a village to raise a child, and sometimes it just takes one dog with a big heart.

Seven months after we said goodbye to Rocky, Zorel and I met a beautiful family from India. The young couple had two children. Zorel, the little boy, and his sister were in a hurry to become friends. So naturally, we adults followed their example. In our conversation, the children's father mentioned he received a beautiful Rocky from his sister. I held my breath, unable to move or say anything. Many minutes passed before I could ask him to tell me more about it.

What I was about to learn reminded me so much of my children. It was like listening to their story in a few meaningful words. It also made me aware that the bond between Rocky and Zorel was stronger than ever. Their sibling love was still very much alive.

As I watched my daughter enjoying her playtime, I could picture Rocky sitting next to me and smiling with his tongue lolling out. She stopped in the middle of their play to show her friends a heart-shaped pendant on the necklace around her neck. Then, with pride in her eyes, she pointed at it. "This is a picture of my brother and me." She put a serious, almost adult-like expression on her face. "You know, dogs can't live very long, but they can love you forever."

According to our new friends, Raksha Bandhan or Rakhi (pronounced Rocky) is the Hindu festival that celebrates love. It is a tradition where sisters tie an amulet called Rakhi around the wrists of their brothers. The knot represents protection and eternal love.

Chapter Six
DREAM CHILD

A good friend is just one call away; a best friend is always next to you.

Two red lines on the pregnancy test proved I was a mom-to-be and that Heaven was and always is for real. A little over a year before I took the test, on July 10, 2012, my grandmother's spirit paid me a visit in a dream and showed me the most beautiful colors I have ever seen, and she transformed my grief into joy. But I was taken by surprise when the colors started fading away and were replaced by many pages full of words, followed by many stacks of books. "What's this?" I heard myself saying. The words that followed seemed to have the power to move everything around me. Even my body appeared to be anywhere but in the bed I was lying in. The answer came. "One of your reasons to continue with your life."

Then an image of a tiny baby was before me. The baby's face didn't look like that of anyone I knew. I first noticed her light brown hair. She most definitely didn't look like me.

When I asked for her name, my grandmother gave me a paper with a name written on it: Zora, meaning "dawn" in English.

"But that's your name," I whispered, still in awe of that precious little human being. "Is this you when you were a child?"

"No" my grandmother answered in the form of written words.

"Me?"

"No!"

"Then who?" I murmured.

"Your daughter," she responded.

"My daughter?" I repeated in disbelief.

My grandmother gave me a quick nod before the colors were replaced with darkness.

When I opened my eyes to a new day, the chandelier above my head was close enough I could reach it. Its electrical ceiling box was detached, and the light fixture's wires were loose. I couldn't help but smile, my thoughts revolving around my grandmother.

My heart was shattered into pieces, and I had no hope, but I wanted to believe everything my grandmother said to me. Her heart spread honesty and truth no matter how close or far. Her heart was full of love for me.

On May 17, 2014, that baby was born. It was a miracle to hold in my arms the beautiful girl who was part of my life even before she was born. She was my miracle sent from Heaven, my pure joy. I named her Zorel Victoria Kostic—her first name is slightly different from my grandmother's, but she has her maiden name. What's more, now she prefers to be called Rose without even knowing that was my grandmother's mom's name. To this day, I call her my dream baby. The dream child her great-grandmother Zora Kostic gifted to me.

The day Zorel turns seven, I believe Heaven is never too far. I believe Rocky will be here to celebrate with us because my grandmother proved to me that once the soul is free from this world and its limits, it can be everything and do anything.

All day, Zorel wears her favorite necklace that displays a picture of Rocky and her. She shows it to anyone who will look. When she blows out the candles on her birthday cake, she whispers, "I wish Rocky would come back." She loves her furry brother. She's showing me what my grandmother had years ago, that Heaven and Earth are interconnected. "Happy birthday, my child. I wish Rocky would come back too. I know he will. I have faith in that."

Watching them grow together was like being taught in a classroom full of life lessons. Whatever they did together, they were in perfect harmony. Even when they were swimming far from one another, sleeping on different sides of the bed, or sticking their heads out of windows on opposite sides of the car. They always shared glances before going back to what they were doing. Those glances melted my heart.

Rocky's last night in his earthly home was spent looking at Zorel. When we returned from our short walk, I watched him decide where to lie down. He seemed to hesitate between two of his favorite spots in the dining room: next to the patio door or in the hallway where he could see her in her bed. So, naturally, he chose the latter. Only days earlier, I begged family members to open their doors for Zorel so she didn't have to watch Rocky's final moments, and I was devastated when my pleas went unanswered. But I was glad she was there for him and me that night. Her presence was his comfort, and it reminded me that she needed one of us to stay with her. To go on with life.

I believe that how much Rocky loved Zorel and how much he cherished every moment he spent with her can't be compared to anything else. No human can love like that. They both showed me that the connection between a child and their dog is like no other as it is a pure heart-to-heart connection. They do not try to be perfect. They want to be simple, to just be. They give us their presence like the most precious gift. But we rarely appreciate this enough until the child is no longer a child, and the dog's paws are not there anymore to follow us to the kitchen, bathroom, and everywhere else we go. We are too busy to notice these priceless gifts are nothing but love.

"I love you, Rocky." I can hear Zorel's voice again. There is excitement in her eyes, and presents are spread across the floor. New toys. Some of them still sitting there unopened. Her eyes hold sadness. This is her first birthday without Rocky, and her little family is broken now. She tells her friends her big brother is in Heaven. She tells me he came into her dream last night.

"He hasn't come into my dreams yet," I tell her.

"Don't worry, Mom. He will come," she assures me.

I give her a massive hug. We both need one. We both miss his wagging tail, wiggling hips, and long, happy howl.

Chapter Seven
BEACH

Dogs make every day of life meaningful.

At the beginning of May 2017, I found a letter attached to my door. The leasing office informed me that I had a prohibited animal on my property. That same day, I learned that the new management was convinced I had a wolf living with me instead of a dog. That gave me an excellent reason for moving from Dallas to Houston with my pack, and I never looked back. The ocean, easily visited from our new location, became our sweetest escape.

I don't know whether our first day at the beach was more exciting for Zorel or Rocky, but I had never seen them happier.

First, we found the least crowded but the most dog-friendly beach in the area. After that, my children were free to chase after everything they came across, whether it was birds, fish, waves, or one another. I spent hours upon hours sitting in the sand

watching them. I could never get enough of that. If there is anything that I can choose to see before I close my eyes on this life, it would be the two of them running on the beach.

Rocky was not the only dog there, so he and Zorel greeted other four-legged swimmers. When they had their fill of that, they played fetch and tug-of-war with sticks. But even that couldn't keep their interest for too long, so they discovered a new game. Shaking water off their bodies around me was something that, I believe, they enjoyed the most. And trying to run didn't help because they were always faster. This prompted them to jump on me and transform me into their surfboard in the sand. In the end, we were all rolling around like naughty little children.

Zorel and I rarely go to the beach now. If we do, we never leave before writing Rocky's name across the sand. While looking at the spots where the sky is kissing the ocean, we hug our boy with our hearts. In my mind, I still hear him barking. I can still see him swimming beside his little sister and herding her in. His paw prints are everywhere I turn.

The beach remains beautiful. Other children and dogs are swimming. Birds are flying, and fish are frolicking. There are so many sticks laying around. I pick one up and write in the sand, "Please come back home. Please, Rocky, come back to us." It feels good to bring back happy memories. It feels good to hope.

The other day, Zorel looked through some old videos on my phone and found one of Rocky and her. I was writing on my laptop when a well-known howl filled our house. I lifted my head, took off my glasses, and turned toward her. The smile traveled from her eyes to her lips as she listened to her voice. "Rocky, Rocky."

Then I heard more of Rocky's howling. That was their beach

time a year ago. In my mind, once again, everything became so real and so alive. They were running around on the sand, swimming against the waves, enjoying life—two of my favorites recorded at the peak of their happiness.

Chapter Eight
HURRICANE

Loving dogs is one of the best things you can do for humanity.

A hurricane hit two months after we moved to Houston. Hurricane Harvey sentenced us and many of our neighbors to stay indoors. For five days, we lived *in* the lake instead of *by* the lake, and the cars around our building looked more like submarines than land vehicles. What mattered most was that we were still alive. And that we had each other. Zorel and I also had our cheerleader, Rocky.

Rocky, as always, made things better. In all that mess, I had to smile each time I tried to encourage him to do his "business" on the patio. He would run away from me and go inside, determined that he would never lose his sense of responsibility and politeness no matter what. He often went to one of the living room's corners and gave me a long stare that said "Catch me if you can."

We had to figure something out, and we did because, with Rocky, there was always some solution. Some days, neighbors helped me carry him to the "less wet" side for a quick potty break. On other days, I carried him myself. So even though that lake was well-known for having snakes and alligators, Rocky and I crossed it like champs.

A couple of days before Harvey cut us off from the rest of the world, we received a letter from our leasing office. They advised us to go to a shelter. The letter also stated that we couldn't take our pets with us. I paid little thought to that, as I knew I would never leave Rocky behind. I had already envisioned myself sitting on our building's roof with both of my children next to me if things took a turn for the worse.

I tried to be optimistic. But unfortunately, that prompted me to think of times when the three of us were face-to-face with death but survived, like when street shooting near our apartment almost killed us while we were sleeping in our home or tennis ball-sized hail slammed down on our car with us inside. These scary moments reminded me that life could end in the blink of an eye.

Hurricane Harvey had many such moments. Still, I knew we would make it through as long as we were together. Neighbors offered a helping hand too. One of them walked through a dirty lake to get to our apartment and watched Zorel while I took Rocky out. Another used his little boat to check on everyone around the neighborhood.

Five days later, the rain stopped, and inch by inch, the water receded. We began seeing more grass and less lake. Soon, Zorel and I could take Rocky out again. We still had each other, and that was what mattered the most.

Chapter Nine
ILLNESS

One act is worth more than thousands of words; people talk, write, and sing about love; dogs show it.

While driving one afternoon, I noticed a pigeon standing by the road and pecking at its food without showing fear of passing cars. Something about that bird made me turn my car around and drive back to where I spotted it. When I parked and walked over to it, much to my surprise, I discovered there wasn't a pile of food in front of it but another bird, whose dead body it was trying desperately to revive. When the pigeon saw me approaching, it moved away but stayed nearby, never leaving its buddy. It was guarding the one it loved.

I walked back to the car and found a plastic bag in my backseat. When I returned, the pigeon was still in the same spot, but its head was tilted slightly this time. It seemed to be waiting for my help. The traffic was picking up and the cars were driving so close to me that I could almost touch them. After scooping the lifeless bird's body inside the bag, I looked back at the pigeon, who observed the entire situation. "I'm sorry, buddy. I know this is not the best option. I know your loved one deserves better." I talked to it in my thoughts, pain marching inside of me. "He's not coming back. Move away from this busy road. Don't get killed. Your friend would not want you to die. Live. For both of you." I walked to the nearby dumpster, my eyes fixed on the ground.

By the time I was back in my car, the pigeon was up on a power line, looking at the spot where its friend had been. Just minutes ago, it wanted to wave goodbye, but its little heart couldn't accept that someone it loved was no longer there. Maybe it waited to see if its little friend would appear or hoped to see broken wings fly again. I didn't know. But I felt its pain. It reminded me that, not too long ago, my hand was stroking my friend—my buddy, my loved one— and I thought I could still feel his warm breath ghosting over my skin. I hoped that once all his pain was gone he would stand up and look at me, and we would go outside, be in the sun, and walk next to each other. Together again.

Now, six months after I put my arms around Rocky for the last time, I try not to blame myself for my mistakes. There were many, but I have two choices: to learn from my mistakes or to repeat them. One of the most essential things Rocky taught me is to appreciate what I have now. By doing so, my grateful heart can replace guilt and resentments with understanding and love. With Rocky by my side, I spent many sleepless nights crying and feeling sorry for myself for not having a family. He was the best family I could ask for, but I kept longing for something different. As some people say "More acceptable by societal standards." We were not a traditional family, but everything in my life was far from traditional. I guess that's why I always wanted so badly to fit in, even at the cost of my peace and happiness. And while I struggled to fit into people's hearts, his dog's heart loved my child and me without any conditions.

I spent most of my years unsatisfied with myself, my life, and the relationships I felt stuck in. I kept finding reasons to make my anger more powerful and more destructive. Then, on June 15, 2018, while I was drinking my afternoon coffee and working on my PhD dissertation proposal, out of the blue, I could no longer move, talk, or breathe. I feared that was it. My four-year-old child and dog would have to watch me die, and nobody could do anything about it. Even worse, there was nobody who would take care of them when I was gone. The latter thought gave me some strength to fight for my life and survive whatever I was experiencing. I knew I needed to stay alive for them.

For the next hour or so, I took cold showers, went to bed and shook under the covers like a frightened child, then found myself again under the cold water. I was still numb but regaining my strength and confidence to move around. I still couldn't talk. My deep breaths were imprisoned behind my rib cage. Somewhere in the background, I could feel that my daughter had been following me around, and I could hear her voice trying to break through a heavy cloud controlling my movements and taking me away. But I couldn't understand one single word. I couldn't understand anything. I felt that my body would hit the floor at any moment, and I would never get up again.

When I gained the strength to open the door and walk down the stairs, I took my daughter and Rocky and walked to the nearest apartment. My neighbor looked puzzled when she saw me. I assumed that my "dead man walking" appearance significantly contributed to that. But I had no time to feel any shame. Knowing that numbness was still in control of my body, I spoke as fast as possible. I told her I didn't know what was wrong with me, but I felt like I was dying, and if that was the case, I wanted someone to know that my girl and my boy had nobody to help them. You can imagine the expression on this poor woman's face. As her eyes widened more after each word crossed my lips, I told her I was maybe experiencing hot flashes, prompting her to place her palm on my forehead. She did so without hesitation. "You are ice cold," she said, shaking her head.

Following this incident, I saw multiple doctors. They diagnosed me with high cholesterol and concluded that I was on the borderline of heart disease. And as for that thing in my head, as one physician pointed out, "Only you know what's going on there." They prescribed pills, one after another, and recommended that I work on reducing my stress.

I had two choices: help myself or leave those I loved the most at the mercy of strangers. I wanted to fight. I wanted to function properly. I wanted to live. Easier said than done. Panic attacks became frequent visitors in my life. My body was falling apart more and more. The stabbing pain in my back kept me in bed. Again, some of my neighbors had to be dragged into my crazy life each time I asked them if they could accompany my little child and her dog on their walk.

Days extended into weeks. Then I could walk and function again. Our team was back on track. In the big, wide world, our small family kept fighting for survival by staying together.

Chapter Ten
ACCIDENT

Nothing is closer to truth and beauty than a dog's eyes—they are like children in play, butterflies in the air, and stars that take the darkness away.

I glanced in my rearview mirror and saw a black Jeep approaching at the speed of light. Darkness soon took over. I found myself in front of a tombstone. I could not see the name written on it. But I didn't have to; I knew it was mine. The date was July 31, 2019.

Many times, I witnessed people losing their sense of hearing last before their transition. That day was no different. My daughter's voice was the last thing I heard. But the sound of it was cut off abruptly. I could no longer see or hear anything and wondered whether she had made it out alive. I had to fight my way back to her just to ensure she was still in a safety seat, awake, and waiting for me to help her.

As I opened my eyes and left a long dark path behind, other senses started returning—all governed by smoke surrounding us. My hand landed on the door, but I couldn't open it. I kept trying without success. I had no time to think or feel anything; I needed to act immediately. I kicked the door with all the strength left in my legs. Two, three, many times before the air from outside started comingling with the helplessness that kept us imprisoned. Zorel, Rocky, and I broke free. We had a long road to recovery before us, but we were ready to begin that journey. More than ever, we needed each other.

Following the accident, I underwent more medical exams and saw more specialists and therapists than at any other point in my life. The majority of them prescribed "happy" pills so I could get over the trauma and pain. When I told them Rocky helped me more than all their prescriptions, their special notes and prescriptions multiplied. What else could they think of me except that I was just another *lost soul*? What else could they do for me anyway? They were not in the ambulance to give me warmth and support by sitting close to me while I held my daughter's hand. They were not with me when my child, despite her own terror, worried about me — "Mom, you're bleeding!" If all the people in this world came together to help me, seven billion of them, with their fourteen billion hands, they couldn't soothe my broken body and heart as much as one dog's paw.

With Rocky always by my side, I realized many people still underestimate the power of listening and the power of 24/7 availability/presence. They are not equipped with powers like that. We humans are not capable of taking time to understand, not without judgment, never-ending lecturing, expectations, ultimatums . . . the list goes on. We can't, not like dogs' beautiful souls.

I had the opportunity to live around and work with those who were quick to label people and dogs as "unwanted" when they aged, became sick, or were seen as too demanding. The same people treated other people and dogs as property they could use, abuse, and throw away. We humans can change and promote change. After all, we all want a joyful, pain-free life and can benefit from dogs' unconditional love. Unfortunately, such love dies each time a dog cries behind bars while waiting to be put to sleep. Rocky was very close to being one of them.

If you follow any animal shelters' social media pages, you will see many dogs who never had an opportunity to show their love or be loved. You can also see those who still have that opportunity. They can make their human a better person and the world a better place, just like Rocky did. I believe dogs are prescribed to us by a higher power to guide us when we feel lost, alone, and unlovable, just like the one who was in the car with me on that fateful day. The only living being who helped my daughter and me cope with the consequences of a major car accident was a four-legged, ex-death row shelter convict. Yes, no one else was there but Rocky. From him, I learned that dogs connect with us with their full-of-love hearts not just empty words. Dogs like Rocky don't give back what we give them—they always give back more and give better.

Chapter Eleven
HOMELESS

There is no place like home; with a dog, you feel at home everywhere.

Some people are prone to homelessness. I am one of them. In 1992, I not only lost my home but also my country. The civil war divided the people and territories of (former) Yugoslavia. For an entire decade, I moved from city to city, from one country to another, filling all sorts of refugee requirements and hoping to find a place to call home. During that time, I only owned things that could fit on me or in my pocket. I didn't mind not having more material things. What bothered me most were relationships that faded and people who were somehow always out of reach. Then I got used to that. It didn't matter anymore that I was walking alone through life. Have you ever seen someone walking next to a homeless person anyway? I haven't. Unless that someone is homeless too or has four legs, a furry body, and a tail.

When Rocky came into my life, for the first time, I was confident that was it. I had a friend who was going to stay. My best friend. I was ready to deal with anything life threw at me, even if that meant being homeless again. And in my case, history repeated itself.

It was the end of summer of 2019, a still hot and humid Texas night, when I took Rocky for a short walk. My daughter was getting ready for bed, so I decided to take my furry child out. Little did I know that soon Rocky and I would become street wanderers.

Those familiar with Texas summers know that humidity is not someone you want as a companion on your walk—especially if you are forced to walk all night long. But on that night, Rocky and I had no other choice. When I found out my daughter had fallen asleep (after she prepared an enormous surprise for me by double locking the already locked door), I assumed we were not getting in for a while.

It was eight p.m., and we had no place to go, as I had no phone, money, or car keys. We also had no water or food with us. After two hours of constantly circling our apartment complex and figuring out how to climb to the second floor, I gave up. "What are we going to do?" I sighed, glancing at Rocky. Being outdoors was in his genes but having an undercoat didn't currently help him. He was probably thirsty, I figured. "We have a long night ahead of us, buddy."

Knocking and ringing the doorbell every five minutes for hours didn't wake Zorel up, so I sat on the stairs next to our door and tried to think. Rocky was next to me, not understanding why we couldn't go in, but as always, he believed in my ability to find a solution. I rested my hand on the soft fur of his neck. This calmed me. New thoughts kept coming. I hoped one of them would turn out to be helpful. Turning my head to the left, I noticed that another apartment's door was ajar. It came to me that I saw the people who lived there moving out just a few days ago. The place was vacant.

As someone who studied law and criminal justice for almost a decade, I never allow myself—no matter what I do—to get to the point of paying a fee to be free. But the will to survive is powerful. I stood up and walked over to the door. Rocky's eyes were fixed on me, and I could read confusion in them, but he followed me. We walked inside. The apartment was empty except for a few paint buckets and trash bags. Water, bathroom, and a/c, things I don't appreciate as much as I should, helped my dog and me survive that night. We laid on the floor and waited for morning. There was nothing to fear or be sad about because we were together. Once again, Rocky made everything better.

That wasn't the first time I stood outside a closed door with Rocky. Many times in my life, I was "displaced" for trusting too much and too soon. But no matter how hungry, scared, or cold my faithful friend was, he always tried to cheer me up. He was there to show me that he believed in me. He knew I would always find us a new home, sometimes even a better one.

Chapter Twelve
PANDEMIC

Dogs need us; we need them more.

It sounds unbelievable to even think that the COVID-19 pandemic could help one realize how powerful and profound a person's desire to leave a beautiful mark on this world can be. But misery is even deeper and more potent. Misery urges you to do nothing but wait for your end.

Before life revolved around being forced to shelter in place or mask mandates, I was an escape artist. I ran away from relationships I didn't feel comfortable in, jobs I was unhappy performing, and my pain. The strongest pain I have ever experienced was watching my dear puppy suffering and leaving this world without me.

When I received Rocky's ashes, I was ready to pack my stuff and escape the apartment, city, and county where everything reminded me of him. But as you can guess, I couldn't.

2020 was not the best year for traveling—not the best to interact with people, period. I had to sit down and do the only thing my heart allowed me to do: cry. I was choking on tears and hurting to the point that I was afraid to get up, feeling as if my entire body would shatter. I kept reminding myself that I had to function because of my six-year-old child. I promised myself that our place would be clean and paid for, there would always be a portion of healthy food on our table, and I would give my daughter some reason to smile every day. Witnessing her grief was the hardest part. I had to find some way to help her. I started reading two books a day to educate myself on how an adult can explain to a child that someone she referred to as her brother and best friend became her guardian angel. I needed to know how to explain that even though she could no longer see Rocky, he was still with her.

I realized I could either go to sleep wishing to die of a broken heart or wake up in the morning and do what Rocky taught me: to be thankful for and enjoy every moment. I chose the latter. I chose to heal. I chose to live. Still, it took me a while to figure out what I needed to do to get where I needed to be. While I waited for a sign from the other side, I remembered the life Rocky and I shared on Earth.

We, the two mutts, had so many things in common. But unlike me, Rocky never let people's ignorance and prejudice affect his love. The love he had was for everything and everyone. He listened with heart and responded with heart. The positive energy around him was undeniable, and even those who didn't believe in dog-human connections were affected by it. It was almost impossible not to notice that smiling face, wagging tail, and loving look in his eyes.

I didn't listen with my heart. I often closed my heart to everyone, including myself. I was cautious around people—seeking solitude for thinking, analyzing, and building strength—but deep inside, I felt exhausted and weak from hurting. I remained prepared to show my teeth if someone put me down.

After eight years in school, where both students and teachers bullied me, I had been through enough. I reverted to a defensive mode. If someone made an insulting remark, I would make ten more. Nicely. Melodically. Poetically.

On the first day of high school, my classmates gave me a nickname: Boxer. A student who threw my backpack on the ground, took my seat, and told me to sit in his lap received a solid right hook to his face. That was part of my promise to myself. I would never let my experiences from elementary and middle school repeat themselves. I became a fighter. I didn't care if someone was bigger, stronger, or angrier than me—I was ready to fight. I didn't feel weak and didn't want to be a victim anymore.

Rocky chose love in any situation, letting me handle people and dogs who were mean to him. I did that gladly. I did anything for my boy. When someone tried to make fun of him for not being purebred, I would stand proudly by his side with my own not-so-purebred appearance. I reminded them that being purebred was just a myth. When nature is forced to produce particular looks and behaviors, "ill purity" is achieved. And for what? I argued. For competition? To put shame on everyone else? To support belief in superiority? I argued that Rocky had unique beauty. Many would turn around and admire his two-colored eyes, shiny three-color coat, and long, circling-around, happy tail. And, of course, that sticking-out tongue that made him look as if he was always smiling was a magnet for people's eyes.

As I had many times before, I longed for a family when the pandemic started. I very much needed one. In difficult times like that, family members and friends try to stick together and help one another, no matter how different they are. But, once again, it was Rocky, my daughter, and me. Nobody else. Nobody to come. Nobody to call. As the world became scarier, I became more anxious. More than ever, it became clear that life is just a candle flickering in the wind, and I feared where my babies would go if fate blew my candle out. I wish I had realized back then what I realize now: I had everyone and everything I needed. Rocky was next to me, sleeping peacefully; my daughter, next to him, playing happily. And my grandma's guiding and loving spirit was always around us. But who can teach a stubborn, ego-powered mind about appreciation? A closed heart couldn't do that.

In Houston, during the early months of the pandemic, every park we regularly visited was closed. So we walked the empty street. We ran in the open fields, Rocky, Zorel, and me. Never having other people around to join us but always having fun with each other, always having love.

Chapter Thirteen
THEY TRIED TO DIVIDE US

Be like a dog—have a simple life and content heart.

Cogito, ergo sum (I think, therefore I am) was coined by well-known French philosopher René Descartes, who lived in the sixteenth century. Descartes believed that dogs, differently from people, couldn't feel pain. To prove his theory, he tortured them in public places. I wish he and all those who shared his belief could have seen the pain in Rocky's eyes when his little sister was almost taken away from us. His pain was deep, both emotional and physical. His pain was real. His pain was hard to bear for those who understand and love dogs.

We all have stories that are too personal to share with others. The following is that story for me. I couldn't write it in first-person voice, so I fictionalized it. This is one tiny slice of a book that I decided to never publish.

With a trembling hand, she opened the door, plagued by the idea of losing the family she had worked so hard to create with her little girl. She needed someone to understand and protect her, someone to care. On the other side stood five men in black uniforms, none of them assuaging her fears. The tallest officer gazed down at her, pinning her where she stood. The shortest on the left, the one with a deep crease in his brow, rested his hands on his hips. He kept glancing over Ashley's shoulder. The remaining three men, older than the other two, kept their lips pursed, their eyes fixed on her face. Would these be the men who destroyed all her hard work, her family?

Ashley didn't want her child to be raised by strangers. That her daughter was still in sight, still sleeping in her bed, soothed the ache she felt. But she worried about the future—there was nobody to ask for any kind of support. She was alone.

"Are you Ashley Martinez?" the tallest officer asked.

Ashley nodded, her stomach tangled in knots. She gathered her courage and asked, "Are you here about last night's shooting in the neighborhood . . . or something else?"

"We received a phone call concerning your child's welfare."

She could feel the blood leave her face. She tried to find the right words, but they stuck to her tongue.

"We just need to see her to ensure she's fine."

Did she really have a choice? Ashley turned, slowly making her way toward her bedroom. First child protective services and now the police. When would they realize that being a single parent didn't mean someone was a bad parent? How could she explain to them that her motherhood had nothing to do with people who used lies to get money from her? Money she didn't have. A loud cry drove a wedge between her and her thoughts. She reached for her child, enveloping the girl in her warm arms.

"Everything'll be okay," she whispered, kissing her forehead. "Everything'll be fine."

Believe it or not, you have free will, free choice, and the right to your opinions, but what you've just read has nothing to do with fiction and all to do with real life. Once again, I had nobody to help me at my lowest low. Yet I had my Rocky. My pain was his pain. Every time I cried, he put his head in my lap and cried with me.

Every time I talked on the phone with a person who demanded money from me, he was beside me, sighing. Each time I shook my head, he moved closer to calm me down. Every time I filed a police report and visited lawyers, he was nearby waiting for me. Without his support, I would never have been strong enough to fight back and keep my family together.

Yes, it's true that when someone falsely accuses you, and you have nobody to validate your claims and no means to get adequate legal help, you can lose everything, including your life. But what they don't know is that when the pure soul of a dog takes you under his protective cloak, you can keep your sanity and be ready to stand tall. One day you may know what I know now, and you may smile, you may cry, you may be in awe, and you may have only one wish —to hug your dog and say thank you.

Dogs don't feel pain like people do; they feel it more. They were born with senses that have a higher vibration than ours. For example, their sense of smell is 1,000,000 times stronger, and their sense of hearing is four times more sensitive. Dogs frequently reach beyond our three-dimensional world. They know life exceeds height, length, and width that we are able to measure. They live it without limiting anything and always giving everything.

Chapter Fourteen

AND THE STORY CONTINUES

Life exists because of love; dogs exist to show us love, the one many people would die for but often die without.

Somebody once told me "When God sees you have no family, he gives you one." Your true godsent family might be a dog. You may be blessed if that's the case. If people shake their heads at this notion, letting them be themselves is the best gift you can give them. Moving on is the best gift you can give yourself.

If you are one of them, do it freely. But also know that in life, where every moment is a first and can be the last, it's a blessing to experience true love—to have someone who loves you without judgment and conditions. Today, I believe God sends you family when you need one, and you get a miracle too. And once a miracle happens, it never ceases; it can't go away. It only gets better when your heart gets powered by belief. It only gets better when your dog leads you back home, back to faith in love.

Somebody also once told me "People don't change people. Dogs do. They reflect your behavior and your entire life to help you realize what areas need improvement. They help you become healthier and happier. They help you find compassion." This resonates with me because I love dogs so much. I trust them more than I trust anyone else, including myself. I think that's why God sent me one—the one who helped me find my real purpose in life.

For many years, I strived to define what faith was. I thought of it as a truth everyone finds inside their heart at their own pace. I was ready to search for it inside of myself. I was prepared to find and add that beautiful symbol of unity to my life. I wanted to believe in something, in anything that didn't serve as a prerequisite for a divided life and divided world. But I couldn't find that one thing.

How could I? People of my nation (former Yugoslavia) loaded their guns while loading their hearts with hatred toward those who had a different way of life and different beliefs. The gunfire was opened, and lives were destroyed. People in my home never showed me that faith in the family is the root of faith in yourself. People in my school didn't teach us about faith in one another. I was married for years without having faith in love.

When Heaven could no longer watch me trying to find my path by bumping into blank signs, it sent me Rocky to save my troubled soul. Only Heaven knew that if people couldn't help me restore my faith in its power, a dog like Rocky could. Heaven knows that once you allow your heart to love a dog, it is an honor and blessing to share your life with him. But not everyone gets this opportunity. Not everyone can change. Not everyone has faith that goes beyond the physical world and what they can see.

We all have guardian angels, but not all of us follow them. Sometimes our skepticism prevents that. Sometimes our heart is closed to accepting messages from above. Angels don't turn their backs on us as we do to them.

I genuinely believe that Rocky is my spirit guide and guardian angel. He became my spirit guide once he took his final breath, but he was my guardian angel since my first breath (more about this in the following chapters).

One difference between a spirit guide and a guardian angel is that a spirit guide can be anyone who transitions from this world to another realm with whom we have a strong connection within this life. But a guardian angel is our soul's source, a piece of saintly beauty we carry within ourselves. Angels never experienced human limitations. They don't know ego or love with conditions. They are simply divine.

The "People don't change people" notion also reminds me of many psychopaths whose powerful negative energy aimed to destroy me. Scientifically, there is no effective approach that can stop these people from inflicting emotional pain on others. Except if a dog steps in and finds that soft spot in them. I witnessed that when they spend time with their furry companion, these people are capable of showing love—true love.

Chapter Fifteen
HOW ABOUT YOUR STORY?

Love a dog and he will love you back. With people there is no such certainty.

As a pet lover, some of your life's happiest moments are spent with your furry, feathered, or scaled friend. And some of the worst moments occur once your friend's spot in your home is empty. Do you believe that the love your pet has for you is here one day and vanishes the next? You likely chose this book because you don't—you can't—and you want someone to validate that feeling that losing a beloved animal companion is like no other loss. The depth of this loss is immeasurable because, contrary to people, animals love without conditions and without judgment. They don't need meditation or prayer to connect with their roots or to keep themselves grounded; they know how to live wholly and holy. They are naturally connected to the mesmerizing universal energy.

Pet loss is unlike any other loss because it also exposes you to tiring explanations. For example, you must explain to your boss that you need some time off because you lost a family member, and then you must prepare yourself for the slight eye roll when they learn that you lost a pet, not a human. You must explain to your therapist (if you are lucky enough to find one ready to learn about pet love and loss) that your dog is not like your child; he or she *is* your child. You must explain to your friends that you lost your best friend, a friend who never left your side. You must explain to your social media followers that a sad face emoji does not lessen your pain.

Intentional or not, you might encounter insensitivity to your grief because our world compares these beautiful, living beings to material possessions. And the world believes we can quickly and easily replace whatever we own. Therefore, you choose silence. And consequently, you grieve alone. But no matter how much it hurts, go with your gut—your own belief along with the love that only you and your pet shared.

This may be hard because when you hurt, some people will try to relate to your pain, and for a while, they might do whatever they can to help you, but many more will take advantage of you. This may be hard to believe, but for some people, the more you suffer, the more they prosper. And sometimes those people run businesses that are considered legitimate and are often highly rated and that affect your life in many different ways (more on this later). Some don't even believe animals belong in your house and your life unless they are on your plate. These same people will never understand why you got your pet in the first place.

You must realize their souls are wired differently from your own. Very differently. Try not to blame them for any of their opinions. Just walk away. The farther you go, the sooner you will know that all that matters is already inside you.

One of the things that matters will be the miracles you have experienced. Many will talk about miracles, but you should look no further than within your heart to find your own miracle. Your heart has the answers to all your questions. Signs of your pet's love are everywhere, but you must be open and willing to see them. They will lead you to your pet long before you cross the so-called Rainbow Bridge. But again, do and believe in what resonates with you. As Dr. Demian Dressler pointed out in his book, *Dog Cancer Survival Guide*, take everything that other people, including me, tell you with a grain of salt.

After all, having a pet in your life is a beautiful experience, a blessing, and a miracle. There is no reason for anything to cease. If you believe your dear one is coming back to you (in a physical form as their spirit is always present), don't let anyone tell you otherwise. Never underestimate your faith.

Never.

Think of this faith as the basis of the first law of thermodynamics—the total energy in the universe is constant. Such energy can be transformed from one form to another, but it can never be destroyed.

If you wish for something beautiful, nobody else has to believe in your wish or approve of it. Your belief creates yearning, but if you are trying to live up to other people's values, you are just fooling your heart. Your wish will come true because it's meant for you, not for somebody else. And what others wish and receive is intended for them. If everyone, just for a moment, were to see the world through someone else's eyes, they would realize that regardless of our different views on life, we all share the wish to hold somebody we lost one last time.

Is anything more real than love? Is there anything impossible with it involved? Keep in mind that pets don't act like people when it comes to love. They never keep their love selfishly for themselves; they share it and spread it around. I like to imagine Rocky's love like rain falling on a fading flower, my grieving heart, the rain that helps the flower find its way back to life.

The only thing pets keep for themselves is pain and suffering because they know there is plenty of that in the world. On the other hand, if you look around, you will notice your fellow humans keep talking about cases of humanity disappearing and the world falling apart. Following their lead empowers negativity, allowing it to conquer our lives.

When you show your pet what love is, they forget about everything else they have experienced, including whatever negative experiences they may have had with people before coming into your life. They dedicate their life to loving you.

Yet despite the benefits of reflection, sometimes it's okay to not worry about those thoughts and beliefs, to do nothing except keep your heart open, be connected to the source of love, and let your beloved pet guide you. They will lead you to a better place before you know it. Rocky leads me in this very moment as I write these words and breathe in his beautiful scent of comfort and love.

Do you remember first seeing your pet and falling in love with them? You have probably thought and talked about that moment on many occasions. But that might not have really been the first time you met them. We may have met our pets earlier in life. Let me tell you how I believe it all began for Rocky and me.

All I knew about Jonny was that he was my first dog. My grandmother and father told me I was too little to remember him. They described him as a beautiful, loyal, and intelligent German shepherd. Jonny joined our family before I was born. I don't know why, but I always thought he loved me so much. In order to stay in his home, Jonny had to stay away from me. That was the rule. He was smart enough to follow that rule. He was also smart enough to know that breaking it could be very costly. He had to choose between two types of torture: never showing his love for me or losing his home.

Jonny's choice was evident on the day when he moved closer to my stroller and gave me a nose kiss. The first and last one. He had to leave his old life behind only a few days later.

The man who took Jonny promised to stay in touch. My father and grandmother told me he grew quite fond of him. He loved to hunt and was delighted to have someone like Jonny to accompany him. A couple of years later, Jonny was accidentally shot and killed by another hunter.

I always felt guilty about Jonny's fate. I was too young to remember much about him, but I loved and felt connected to him, especially in my adult years when Rocky became the most valuable part of my life.

Throughout the years, it occurred to me that Rocky and Jonny shared some similarities. Jonny was a full-blooded German shepherd who was adopted directly from a breeder in Germany. The man was my father's good friend, so he ensured a new addition to our family was the best of the best. Rocky was a husky and Shar-Pei mix, but I never did genetic testing on him to discover his breed makeup. Interestingly, many people, including vets, tried to convince me he had more German shepherd in him than any other breed. I didn't think or care much about that. He was perfect for me, no matter what breed mix he was. I was very proud of his "pure-mixed breed" and that both his and my appearance had people guessing what we were, where we came from, and so on and so forth. What I cared about was that I had always felt he became part of my life long before I saw him at the Dallas adoption event.

After Jonny, three dogs lived in our household, and many more strays came in for food and temporary shelter—all small dogs. Although I loved all of them, my inner voice reminded me that I am a big dog person. When Rocky came into my life, I felt that was it. I knew I had found the one I was looking for. Rocky, too, from day one behaved like my home was where he belonged. But as a human who often sought instant gratification, I started having doubts. I wanted a furry friend who would follow me everywhere, not a puppy that wanted to lead me.

So I didn't disagree for long when my then-husband decided Rocky was too much work and too big for our little apartment. I wasn't happy about returning him to the rescue group I adopted him from, yet I gave in. *Why take on that extra work and extra responsibility?* I tried to convince myself I was okay; I was busy and needed no attachments. Attachments require emotions, and I was taught all my life that emotions were no good. I started thinking about the past. I didn't want it to repeat itself.

I remembered times when I was on a hunt for a book publisher for my work, determined to chase my childhood dream. For years, I reviewed every submission rule I came across carefully, hoping to discover one with requirements I could meet. But none of those publishing houses were interested in any type of "emotional writing." In response, I wasn't interested or willing to starve and fall behind on my bills, so I decided to take a break from my search and find a "real job." In fact, I found three of them. I became a certified pharmacy technician, veterinary technician, and bookstore sales associate.

As a new hire, I received a training manual from each employer. Besides policies and procedures, "emotion display rules" were also listed. The latter were useful when applied to negative emotions one could bring into the workplace. Or so I thought. Soon I discovered those rules covered all emotions. While doing my duties and interacting with other employees, I learned that being physically present was what counted. Of course, your mind was to be used as well, but your heart, only in a reserved manner.

Taking a creative writing course might help me express my emotions on paper, I thought. So I started looking for one and soon found a perfect match. My enrollment and dedication to learning followed. I had an excellent teacher who liked to share his writing in class while encouraging us to share our pieces. As a shy student who was very concerned about her English-as-a-third-language accent, I often asked him to read my poems for me. He did. One day, upon finishing one of them, he proclaimed that I was a so-called emotional writer. I didn't dare ask if that was good or bad. I just smiled and thanked him.

I still felt unfulfilled and decided to abandon something I had a passion for. Yes, once I realized what was valued in the world around me, I closed my heart and stopped writing. With that, I allowed my dream to die.

But that day, when I was looking at Rocky sitting in front of me and begging me with his sad eyes not to take him back, I started reevaluating many decisions I had made. That brought back emotions and values buried inside me. Those which I promised myself many years ago would be forgotten, always safely hidden from others. I finally decided to cherish what I loved, knowing he was not going anywhere. He would be at my home, where he needed to be.

Day after day, as Rocky grew bigger, my desire to just be myself grew with him. Still, I didn't know whether Rocky's presence would be enough to help bring out the best in me. I didn't know my puppy's unconditional love and trust in me would help me realize that what other people have to say is not so important, especially if their reasoning is not sound to my heart. They are entitled to their opinions, and I am entitled to my life.

My life was shaped by a hero called Rocky, who didn't let me or my emotions die. Because of him, my daughter is not alone today. She still has someone to love her—her mom. Because of him, a dog peeked inside the stroller carrying me and inside the stroller carrying my daughter. She is growing bigger; I am getting older. Both of us know another dog is waiting for us. Somewhere. He, too, is bringing that special part of Rocky. His heart. His love. Because of him—today, right now—I do what I love. I write about him.

Chapter Sixteen
WORKING BESIDE ROCKY

Sometimes you may wish to have a passion for a simple task, just like your dog has when he closes his eyes and scratches himself behind the ears.

Seven billion people couldn't save one human's life, but one dog could. It all began on May 17, 2008, when a woman visited an adoption event, pointed at a sad-looking puppy in a small cage, and said, "This is the one I want." She returned home thinking she had rescued him. And she did. Once. But he saved her more times than she can remember.

In 2010, she was rescued from domestic violence, which almost ended all her dreams and her life. In 2012, she was rescued from drowning in a sea of grief after losing the most important person in her life. In 2014, she was rescued from someone who promised a life full of love but gave her life without parole. In 2018, when she became ill and had nobody to take care of her, she was rescued by him—her loyal companion brought her back to life. In 2019, she, her dog, and a five-year-old child were in a car when another driver ran a red light and almost killed them. Once again, he never left her side and helped her put together the broken pieces of her body and heart.

Today, Rocky—who was once a four-month-old puppy on the euthanasia list—and I volunteer together with a local ministry. He listens when people talk and children read. He does it with cuddly affection and eyes full of joy; his heart is always ready to embrace with love.

This is Rocky's story, the story I want to share with the seven billion people of this world, people who are sometimes too busy with their own lives to notice anyone else. That's why the universe sends us precious heroes like Rocky, who remind us we are not alone.

In 2020, when I nominated Rocky for the "Hero Dog Award," the American Humane Society published this story (along with Rocky's picture) on their website. Rocky was in the "Shelter Dogs" category, and I believed he had a good chance of winning. Silly me; I didn't realize voting would be based on the nominator's marketing skills and social media followers rather than the dog itself. I still felt a sense of joy each time someone sent me an email that read "I voted for Rocky."

My hero never stopped working to help others. His specialty was being around children. He became a therapy dog for a Houston-based non-profit organization called "Faithful Friends." I accompanied him to schools, libraries, and many "good cause" events. When sitting beside children who struggled in any area of learning, Rocky was patient, full of understanding and kindness (he often sniffed children's faces and hands when they were shy and nervous), and was free of any kind of judgment. They repaid his sweet nature by reading him as many stories as they could, petting him as long as they sat by his side, and bringing him as many treats as they could carry in their little hands.

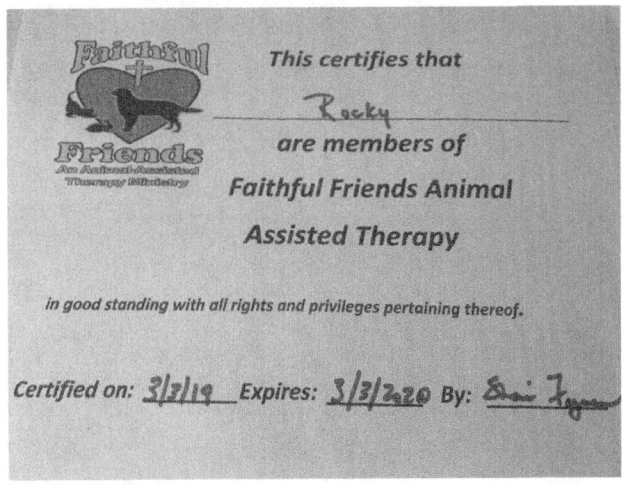

Rocky, Zorel, and I visited libraries on our own as well. Children were excited to meet the main characters from the book *Rocky and a Girl with a Curl*. During those readings, they also had an opportunity to meet and adopt one of our fosters. And Rocky fostered many dogs, keeping up well with his mom, who often found strays and brought home shelter underdogs (dogs who were likely to be put down). Like that wasn't enough, he adopted a guinea pig that someone left at a pet store. It was January, the month when people got rid of unwanted animals they received for Christmas—the perfect season for Rocky to rescue another furry fellow. Not long after, he also adopted a cat that was found along with four other cats inside a sealed box in the middle of the street.

ROCKY

His house was one big rescue. His mom was rescued as a baby by her grandmother. His human sister rescued his mom later in life. His furry brothers, cat Pumpkin and guinea pig George, were rescued from unloving homes. His entire family was rescued by him.

Rocky's work didn't end there. After our car accident, he became my PTSD therapy dog and my ESA (Emotional Support Animal). He took that role with such seriousness and pride. When I put a collar and leash with the "therapy dog" sign on him for the first time, he lifted his head high and led me outside, just like many years ago when he was a puppy. Yet this time, he didn't pull me like his mission was to catch anything that moved. He led me because he knew I had to find a way out of trauma and fear. He knew he was my guardian angel before I knew the true meaning of these words.

Chapter Seventeen

RESEMBLANCE BETWEEN DOG AND HIS PERSON IS MORE THAN PHYSICAL

Somebody once told me that teaching is the most important job in the world because everyone needs a teacher. I chose the best one out there: Dog.

Soon after my birth, my parents separated and left me behind with my paternal grandmother. When I turned six and started going to school, I was eager to make friends and learn about the wonders of life. I could never have guessed my teachers and classmates would bully and physically abuse me for the next eight years. To them, I was just an ugly orphan. I was the smallest and darkest child in my nondiverse class. My tiny, egg-shaped face was ornamented with a big nose and a much bigger frown. I kept my eyes fixed on the ground and tried not to cry when I heard "I hate her," "she's so stupid," "look at her," and "look at what she's wearing."

My old and cheap clothing made my time spent in school even more unbearable. I heard hurtful remarks everywhere I turned. In the classroom, my teachers didn't protect me. Instead, they often joined my classmates when they mocked me. Children avoided me as if I had some highly contagious disease. Teachers treated me as an excellent candidate for becoming a career criminal in the future.

Silence was my only refuge. It had a long, opaque veil that could cover all my pain. I didn't say a word, even when I learned the material in the textbooks from cover to cover. I preferred getting Fs and beatings from teachers. Physical punishments didn't take as long to be meted out as emotional ones. Standing in front of the class in a clown-like fashion or in a corner next to the trash can was much more painful than bruises that came from pushing and slapping. Boy, that shaming truly hurt. It made me think of running away and never returning to that awful place. But I was afraid to move. Afraid to breathe. Afraid to hope that one day someone would care about how I felt.

As for recess, while everyone else in school looked forward to it, I wished it never existed. I sat on a bench alone in the cafeteria and watched everyone else eating their meals. Then I sat on a side road in the playground and watched them play. I never had spare money in my pocket to buy one of the loaves of bread with some cheap spread they sold at school. I was hungry and scared. Nobody paid attention to me.

In our neighborhood, I had no friends. Things worked like this: if my grandmother wasn't on good terms with a child's parents, the parents didn't allow their child to play with me. My grandmother was a loner, and I had no choice but to follow her path.

The older I grew, the lonelier I felt. I started finding and appreciating the company of stray dogs and cats. I felt that my life resembled their lives. My father brought me a few dogs, but they didn't stay in our house for long. Rija, a beautiful black poodle, got lost; Maggie, my little Pekinese, was hit and killed by a car; and Duki, my other Pekinese, didn't survive the war that devastated our country.

The beginning of Rocky's life was not happy either. Soon after his birth, he found himself at a high-kill animal shelter in Dallas,

Texas. Because of the lack of space, he ended up on a euthanasia list. This was in 2008 before the social media "explosion" happened. At that time, it wasn't possible to share posts about shelter dogs in need and ask locals to foster or make pledges and contact rescues for dogs they wanted to save. Dogs were dying behind closed doors, in cold rooms, and nobody but those who ordered their euthanasia and those who put them to sleep knew they had ever existed.

I often imagined a cold shelter cage with a little puppy in it. A hungry puppy. A scared puppy. The puppy everyone could bully and nobody understood or wanted as a friend. Like when I was a child, sitting behind the school bench and feeling the same way. Rocky didn't know if he would survive another day in the shelter; I didn't know if I would survive another day in school.

Rocky was a beautiful pooch—the most unique one I had seen—and I had worked with dogs all my life. But people have their opinions about big dogs with big heads, long snouts, and dark fur, as they have their opinions about dark, long-nosed kids. They often classify unwanted dogs as potential wolves (big, dark-colored dogs experience the lowest adoption rates) and unwanted kids as future welfare recipients or criminals. Societies all around the world tend to approach both groups with caution. And while there is nobody to help them overcome their hunger and fear, hope is still in their heart, hope they will find someone who may see them differently.

According to the rescue group that pulled Rocky out, a shelter informed them that a handsome little fellow was about to die. The lady running the rescue begged for an extension but was given only until the end of the day to come and pick him up. When she received an email with Rocky's picture, she was devastated that such a beautiful, healthy puppy wouldn't make it out alive. She did everything possible to make it to the shelter on time. By the end of that day, Rocky was out. A beautiful, healthy, and happy dog was waiting for me. Around the same time, miles away, I realized I had no friends. I needed one. Soon. Yet I was wondering where to look for someone who would understand where I was coming from. Up to that point, I had met nobody with similar life experiences. Nobody could relate to the fear of abandonment I was living with.

Years later, every time I would tell Rocky—and I used to talk to him about everything—that we would not see each other for a while, either because I needed to travel back to my home in Europe or because I needed to run errands, his eyes filled with sadness. The light in them disappeared, and they were no longer blue but dark like the sky before the rain comes. In moments like that, he preferred to rest his head in my hands and wait for whatever I was going to tell him next. "Don't worry! I'll come back to you, Rocky. Always." His sigh of relief was all that mattered to me.

Rocky visited animal shelters with me a few times. He didn't mind going in. Some memories probably reminded him that places like that were filled with the sickening stench of fear and death. He hesitated at first, but then he followed me in. He trusted me when I told him we were picking up a foster dog. Soon I read joy in his eyes because another shelter dog was joining the free world. That also meant he was getting a new playmate for a while. Life couldn't be any better.

One day, three decades after my school years in Bosnia and Herzegovina ended, I was sitting next to Rocky in my living room and staring at my laptop screen. I needed a career change but didn't know where to start looking. With three college degrees and one PhD in progress, I soon discovered I was overqualified for some jobs and inexperienced for many others. But then one particular job caught my attention. One of the well-known community colleges in the Houston area was looking for an Adult Education/English as a Second Language (ESL) Instructor.

You are crazy were the first words that came to my mind. *School is where many of your childhood traumas happened; besides, you have a thick accent.* I tried to convince myself I was not a good fit. *Close that page and move on; just move on.* I kept talking myself out of applying. *You can't do it. You are not good enough. Your knowledge and your education are for nothing. Everyone will make fun of you just as they did years ago.* I didn't realize that while different thoughts were coming to my mind, I started filling my information in. When I was done, I took a deep breath, glanced at Rocky, and clicked the "Submit" button.

A couple of months later, I walked into the classroom as a professor and fell in love with my job. When I stepped inside the school for the first time, I was like Rocky stepping inside the shelter. I was hesitant and afraid, and my heart was heavy with painful memories. But just like Rocky, I knew I needed to go in in order to make a difference in someone else's life. I was also making a difference in my own life. I realized love makes everything possible.

With Rocky by my side, I also worked on and published my first book. He always encouraged me to live and do what I love—not tomorrow, next week, or next month, but right now. With him, I didn't have to be ashamed of my broken English. I didn't have to worry why editors who promised a bunch did very little to help me. I didn't have to wait to take a baby step to get closer to where I wanted to be. With him, I knew even if nobody ever understood what *the author was trying to convey*, I would have to believe in myself as he believed in me.

Again, my guardian angel Rocky gave me the strength to step out of my comfort zone as well as my victim zone and start believing in myself. He taught me there is no love without peace and no peace without forgiveness. For me, forgiving starts every time I come face-to-face with my imperfections. It starts with forgiving myself for having bad days, making poor decisions, and saying words I should never say. As the Hawaiian ho'oponopono prayer goes: "I'm sorry. Please forgive me. Thank you. I love you."

ROCKY

I'm sorry, Rocky, for every time I cried over people who were not worthy of my tears. Instead, I could have enjoyed the peace our walks gave me. Please forgive me for not kissing those silky soft ears of yours more. Thank you for loving me unconditionally. Many people will live and die without experiencing that kind of love. I love you. Only because of you do I know the true meaning of these words.

Chapter Eighteen
LISTEN TO YOUR DOG; I WISH I DID (MORE OFTEN)

People teach dogs tricks; dogs teach people how to be real.

What in life is more predictable than our daily routine? We wake up, go to the bathroom, go to the kitchen, eat, get dressed, go to work, and go to sleep. Repeat everything the next day. The next month. The next year. If you are lucky enough to have a dog or any other pet next to you, you should and would include them in your routine. Take them for a walk, feed them, groom them, and repeat everything the next day. But if you pay attention, you will see that your pet adds something essential to your life, and that's snuggling that can take you out of that endless cycle. Those snuggles make everything better, enjoyable, and out of the ordinary.

While being licked from your chin to your forehead, you realize that simple moments in life are precious and they bring you peace. Peace leads to understanding. Understanding leads to compassion. Compassion leads to love that connects one heart to another, like the heart of the dog that spreads love to help people in need. That heart would fight until its last beat for those it loves. It would go way beyond anything you thought it could do.

ROCKY

I thought I listened to Rocky and lived my life according to his teachings about patience, forgiveness, and kindness. I was wrong. On July 15, 2018, I became like a fish that tried to swim on land. With no one to help me back into the water, just like that fish, I was gasping for air and dying.

During that time, many of my days started—and many of my nights ended—with panic attacks. Sometimes I experienced them during my walks with Rocky. I went from cheerful to unable to move and breathe. My heart beat on my inner walls and begged for more time; my eyes were fixed on Rocky. In all that misery, I thanked God for letting me see my dog's face, the face that spread peace and love. Rocky often became as still as a statue when this happened, probably thinking about how he could save me. His presence did much more than both of us realized. It was a miracle.

I felt like I was knocking on death's door, but I felt better with Rocky next to me. I knew I wouldn't die alone if I did die, and my daughter would still have her best friend to share her life with. I believed that nobody and nothing would separate Zorel and Rocky, even without me around. But, like he was reading my mind, Rocky didn't want to let go of me. He wanted me to fight. He wanted me to stay alive. During those episodes, he often moved closer to me and kept his eye on me until a heavy load fell off my shoulders. In one moment, I was in a sinking ship, crying hopelessly, and in the next, my rescuer pulled me to the shore, and I was peaceful, loved, and happy to be there.

Yes, I had no family to take care of me or tell me everything would be okay, but I had more than that. I had somebody who never pointed out how imperfect I could be but always pointed out how important I was to him.

People say parents allow children to step on their shoulders so they can have a better life. That's what Rocky has done for me. It was like living my life in a plane cabin where the air pressure was too low, so he kept putting the oxygen mask on for me. He wanted me to live and fly high because he was the only one who loved me more than he loved his own life. He never had any hesitation. He never had any philosophical dilemma over who most deserved to live and be happy. Only he believed in my dreams and inspired me to have dreams bigger than myself.

American research scientist Marcel Vogel believed any child raised without love was deformed. As a child and an adult, I longed for love from people. I longed for someone to tell me, "Don't worry, I am here." Can you imagine how I felt once I realized my dog gave me a gift like no other, one of unconditional love? Can you imagine how I felt once I realized I could do everything those who bloomed in love could do? Everything changed for me when I learned that my scars don't define me. The road before me is still long, but I am moving forward.

Today, when I think of everything I put my daughter and Rocky through, I want to scream at the top of my lungs. Especially for Rocky, who paid the ultimate price. The negative energy I spread affected his pure soul. My imbalance became his own. While I accumulated more anger that served my purpose of being unforgiving, he became weaker. While I spent many years of my life playing that old sad movie called the past inside my head, Rocky spent his life showing me my blessings. He wanted to show me that if I had grown up with my parents, had many friends, and had a happy marriage, my life would be very different. But his loving soul and my darling child might then never be part of it; they are my blessings, my biggest blessings.

After watching his painful departure from this world, one thing that keeps me going is his lesson that choosing love over anything else can cure me. He lived with this beautiful mission, and I want to do the same. So instead of blaming myself, I focus on sharing

RUBY (SPRINGER SPANIEL).—STACY SMITH, SAN DIEGO, CA

"**H**ere we are, two different *species*, but we have this deep connection, one that's been going on for centuries, ever since the first wolf and the first man decided to hang out together. It's kind of beautiful: not-furry and furry, one who talks and one who doesn't, two-legged and four-legged. But relying on each other."
—Deb Caletti

21·Wednesday·May *2025*

Rocky's lesson of love with others. By doing this, I can strengthen my compassion for the world in and around me.

Rocky picked up on my emotions and tried to help me realize I couldn't keep going like that. Not if I wanted to live. I just didn't know what to do to survive. Because of that, he showed me where I was heading to. Just a few months before Rocky was diagnosed with cancer, I hung a picture on a wall that said *Enjoy Every Moment*. Rocky's favorite spot was under it. It was as if he was saying to me "Enjoy life, don't hate it." I was so absorbed in my negative thoughts that I didn't allow myself to notice anything else. But each time he moved closer to me, and I could feel his warm breath caressing my skin, I reminded myself to cherish the beauty because it passes so quickly.

I can't turn back time. I can no longer wake up to those beautiful blue eyes looking at me and begging me to turn my life around. But I can take what I've learned from Rocky and follow more principles of love than ego for the rest of my life. Neither my life nor I will ever be perfect, but I don't strive for perfection. I strive to be more receptive to the simplicities of life. I finally understand that every moment, something, somewhere begins, and something, somewhere ends. Life doesn't remain the same, and it shouldn't. But that doesn't mean that the joy of living is limited by the time and space that are part of our comfort zone. Our thoughts limit it. We can reach for that joy or not. We can let it embrace us or push it away. We can continue to love no matter what, or we can never allow our hearts to love again. It's our choice.

These days when I close my eyes, I call Rocky's name in my mind and remember our happy times. I feel that the life we live in our bodies is nothing compared to the energy of the universe that can unify all energies and all souls. But if souls feel imprisoned, the energy that connects them to the higher power becomes blocked. That's when real suffering takes over.

While I was desperately trying to see Rocky in my dreams and looking for any angel-like sign from him, once again, I was unaware that everything he did was for my and my child's sake. My pain and constant tears were overwhelming for him. They were breaking his wings each time he tried to spread them. It was so unfair toward my best friend. So unfair toward me and everyone else around me.

I don't see him, but I feel his presence. Energy flows through my body as soon as I close my eyes and try to do my daily meditation. And then there is his head resting in my lap, falling asleep with me, like my Rocky did when he was a tiny puppy. I place my hand there. I pet his soft fur once again. When I step outside, possums cross my path often, as if Rocky chases them. I chase them too. I have to. The invisible shiny golden leash connects me and my handsome boy.

My daughter was six years old when my grief from losing my best friend started. What do you think happens to a child who has only her mom in her life? You can only guess how and where she would end up if I gave up on my life. Rocky knew this better than anyone else, so he pushed me away to push me up. My wise teacher, my loyal buddy, my rock, never gave up on me and never let me down. He believed in me and waited for me to connect with the universe where he was running, happy and free.

Every day, I look forward to hearing from him. Messages come in different forms. Sometimes I see a coin on the ground that grabs my attention. Sometimes a feather rests on my car when I approach it. Sometimes a butterfly tries to land on me. Sometimes his bark wakes me up. Sometimes we are on our way to the dog park and everything around us feels like more than a dream. There is nothing more real than this love between us. I often think about what he would communicate to me the next time I see him running to meet me. Whatever it's going to be, it will be my blessing.

It feels good to surrender worries, to trust, and just go with the flow. About seventy-one percent of the Earth is covered with water.

More than sixty percent of the human body is water. Water creates new paths in life and takes us where we need to go. Water keeps us alive. But love brings us the joy of living. Every morning when I open my eyes, Rocky's love embraces me.

Chapter Nineteen
HOPE

There is a lot one should remember about their dog. There is much more one should forget about people.

What now? Asking this question became my habit. What to say when Zorel asks me, "Mom, can you tell me a story about Rocky because I miss him and I am so sad?" How, when I share her feelings? How do I chase her in the park when I just want to sit and cry? Even if I try, I will never match Rocky's playfulness.

What now when we moved out of Houston because every place there reminded us of the happy times we spent with Rocky? Beach. Park. Zorel's school, where Rocky volunteered as a therapy dog. The bus stop where he waited every day for her to come home. The pet store where everyone knew the leader of our pack. Nature trails where we chased deer, possums, and raccoons. Our apartment that felt like home only because of him.

What now when, in a new city, we still cry old tears? What now when there is so much we want to share with him in this physical world, but we can't?

I went back to writing this book and kept sharing what I

learned from Rocky. Zorel, my little extrovert, wasted no time making new friends and telling them all about her beautiful puppy. That's what we did to rebuild our lives. We are starting over and bringing Rocky wherever we go. He is more than a part of our memories. He saved and shaped our lives and gave us a family and hopes we wouldn't have had without him.

Rocky opened my eyes about everything I was doing wrong in my life. The guilt's grip is firm, mainly because I didn't love myself more during our earthly time together. That would have made him happy. If I had, I would have had more love for others, most importantly for him and my daughter.

Through his interactions with people and animals, Rocky showed me happiness doesn't depend on how accepting others are of us. Happiness is being true to yourself and never trying to be something you are not.

When it comes to how Rocky interacted with people and dogs, he was never a fighter. He always wagged his tail even when people tried to avoid him or push him away because he was "too big" or other dogs attacked him because he was too playful. I was the complete opposite. I was always ready to argue and hold a grudge when someone did me wrong. But he never judged me for that. He was the only living being who did nothing to make me feel unloved.

In all those years we spent together, I was blind and deaf to his efforts to show me what matters in life and what doesn't. I didn't want to change and live a different life. I didn't want to try stepping out of my comfort zone. Mountains of pain surrounded me, pain I had gotten used to. The more I used anger as a getaway, the quicker I became addicted to it. When Rocky tried to help me from the "other side," I realized he was still with me, still trying to show me I deserve better from this world, and this world deserves better from me.

Whenever my guardian angel Rocky comes to me, I know

everything is connected, linked to love. And he comes to me every single day. When I close my eyes and focus on my breathing, I feel a pulsing all over my body. The smile on my face proves that this buzzing sensation is the energy he uses to touch my soul. That feeling is beyond any beautiful emotion I have ever known. If you are a believer, just open your heart and see that the love you think you lost is still with you. Untouched. Unchanged. The deepest of all.

I truly hope you find that feeling and just go with it, wherever it takes you. I read somewhere that about ninety-five percent of the ocean is still undiscovered by humans. Now, try to compare that five percent of the ocean humans have already observed and mapped to happiness and meanings someone brought into your life before moving to a higher realm. You can only imagine how much joy they can still bring you to help you live a more fulfilling life. It is endless.

During my connections with Rocky, I learned that when we live in the lower, material-based realm, we believe that while we are here, we can do it all, and when we are gone, we are done. We don't want to think that the spirit is not tied to the physical world. It is limitless. Free. We don't want to believe that we are all spirits more than we are our bodies, and many of us choose to be dragged down by the body's desires rather than raised by the spirit's love. We don't want to think of spirit at all. Period. That's why spirit love remains unexplored. That's why our lives remain attached to what is around us instead of what is inside us. That's why we see death as a permanent end rather than the beginning of infinity. If you don't believe in the beauty of love, nothing and nobody can make you beautiful. If you don't believe in miracles, a miracle will happen to someone else instead of you. If you stop hoping, you can still find something —anything—to hope for. But you must try. Then more reasons to hope will come. Don't turn them down. Let them in.

It took me a long time to learn that Rocky didn't just go and take with him all that he was giving me all his life. He didn't leave me alone and scared (even though I felt that way in the early stages of my grief). Without him. Without love. He knew cords of love couldn't be broken. In love, the soul doesn't disconnect from another soul; it is not a phone line that gives you a disconnected call tone when you are trying to get a hold of someone you miss dearly. But like a phone call, long distance doesn't mean that the connection will be poor. A poor connection happens only when we are not paying attention to the one on the other end of the line.

Speaking of the phone, since my daughter was born, my dear mobile device has lost its voice to silent mode. I prefer vibration over a ringtone. This "nudge" always seemed the more natural way to reach out to somebody. So three months into learning to meditate, shortly after closing my eyes and inviting deep breathing to fill my body with peace, I started experiencing something that reminded me of a phone's vibration. I still do. Every day. It is a warm flow of energy, a gentle tingling I feel from my head to my toes. It brings a smile to my face, a smile only Rocky could bring. I know this is him saying "I'm here, calling you. I know you are listening. You know I'm right here with you. I'm reminding you how much I care about you and love you. Turn the radio on and listen to your favorite Stevie Wonder song 'I Just Called to Say I Love You' and you will know what I mean."

It took me a lot of effort to admit there are many things I want to find out, but I will never be able to. Some of them are when, why, and where I will take my last breath. But this breath that I am taking right now is by far more important than that last breath. And this breath tells me to always, always follow my heart.

Rocky guides me every day: Through books that catch my attention when I need to learn something new. Through songs that come on the radio right when I need some cheering up. Through people with dogs I come across when I need a reminder that my eyes see two beings connected by a leash, but my heart sees two beings connected by love. What is before my eyes is temporary; what is in my heart is everlasting.

No, Rocky didn't give up on me. I feel his beautiful spirit everywhere I turn. Because he never stops sharing his lessons of kindness with me, I am opening my heart and learning. Learning to embrace what I have. Learning not to fear what is coming. Learning to tell my daughter every day how much I love her. Learning to show her how to take every moment of life and dance with it, just like Rocky taught me.

Now I see a big difference in her behavior because we are becoming closer every day. We smile and laugh more. We hold hands more often. She told me how much she enjoys my silliness. She seeks adventure and fun. We find them together. It helps her grow. It helps her experience freedom and carelessness. She did that with Rocky. She loved that. We keep our little family together. Our family is the love we share with each other. Our family is Rocky.

Months after Rocky's transition, I had my first dream of his return. In it, Zorel was swimming. I was sitting on one of the largest rocks on the beach, watching her, as I had done many times before. Out of the blue, she screamed, turning around and flapping her arms. I stood up and noticed she was no longer alone in the water. But I wasn't concerned. It thrilled me to see her now jumping up and down in excitement, extending her hands toward me. I smiled before she could look at me and say anything. "It's Rocky. Mom, Rocky's back."

Days before Zorel's seventh birthday, she waited for Rocky. She spoke about him. She waited some more.

She's still too young to understand when I tell her that Mom needs to work on herself a lot more before her furry brother returns. Mom needs to work on parenting with love instead of parenting with impatience and rules. Then her beloved Rocky can return, and we can be a family again. An untraditional family, but a very loving family.

ROCKY

We were the family that spent holidays in the dog park playing fetch. Or swimming. Or walking. Or just lying on the floor, kissing each other's faces, scratching each other's backs. Rocky was next to Zorel until she could find all those spots that needed a good scratch. Then he would move closer to me and let me give him deep belly rubs. Having all fours in the air was all he wanted and all that mattered.

We never cared about having a dining table set as we often sat on the floor with our plates in front of us. We ate there and talked to each other; we felt comfortable. We had no television either. Just piles of books, bags of treats, and snuggles.

In my heart, I carry hope for those experiencing pet cancer. I want to share with them what we went through. This may aid them in making some of their decisions. I had very little time to make mine, which, hopefully, will not be their fate—your fate.

Rocky was a healthy dog, or better said, very resistant to environmental dangers and stress, which was the norm in our home. I was always so proud to count his mixed-breed blessings and believed that cancer happened to other dogs but would never happen to my boy. Most of the time, he was fed human-grade food; he was well-exercised, well-groomed, and showered in kisses. I was in disbelief when the vet told me cancer had spread throughout his body. They recommended euthanasia right away, and I, of course, refused. I took him back home and told him, "We got this." The fighter in me wanted to believe.

It seems like it was just yesterday. I was outside, sitting in my car. We were six months into the pandemic, and vet hospitals, unlike pediatric clinics, didn't allow people to accompany their furry children inside. Once again, the world didn't understand that people can love their adopted children the same as their biological children; looks or species are irrelevant. The vet informed me over the phone that Rocky was terminally ill with lymphoma. I cried as soon as she broke the news; I cried after I hung up. Zorel was sitting in the back seat. She didn't ask questions. She understood. She just said, "Mom, you're not alone; you still have me."

What followed was one vet appointment after another. One holistic approach after another. I tried to educate myself, but I had to do it fast. I fought. He fought harder. His will to stay alive was big and strong, like a mountain. He wanted to stay with his little sister and me. He didn't want us to go through life alone. We couldn't imagine life without him. We didn't want to even think about it. But when you're that desperate, it's hard to stay away from people who try to use your situation for their personal gain. Unfortunately, you can become an easy target for them without realizing it. I did.

From September 18, 2020, to Rocky's transition on November 10, 2020, I read every book and article on cancer I could find and contacted every "healer" I came across online. Besides steroids, I started giving him supplements and CBD with THC oils. He was on ozone and laser therapy. Nothing helped. At least, not long-term.

I buried my head in books. With a cure seemingly out of reach, I wanted to know everything I could about prevention, early symptoms, and available treatments.

This is what I learned:

Dogs are very good at hiding their discomfort and pain until their illness progresses and their bodies start showing the symptoms. They do this because they want to please us. They don't want us to worry. They want, without interruptions, to continue their journey right beside us. From the beginning to the end of their lives, they focus on their love for us more than on their own needs. Thinking about your pup or any other pet silently suffering is heart-wrenching. Yes, they do that. And they continue to do that until the end.

Human-grade, non-processed food is safer for them. Isn't it true that food used for human consumption, despite all regulations, is often recalled? That said, if the dangerous substances "accidentally" end up in food for those who can press charges, I can only imagine their quantity in food that is designated to those defined by law as property. Nothing can replace a home-cooked meal, regardless of how promising dog food appears. At least you know the food's ingredients. One important thing to note is that not everyone is willing to educate themselves about what kind of human food is good for dogs and what is not. By no means do I recommend to anyone to feed their pet whatever they eat. If you don't want to learn about what food is beneficial for them, don't try it at all because you can do more harm than good. Remember, many foods that are healthy for us are poisonous or not tolerated well by dogs. Like people, dogs can have food allergies. The process of starting to feed your pet human-grade meals is similar to becoming vegan or vegetarian yourself. If you don't educate yourself about what nutrients your body needs and how to get them from a plant-based diet, the benefits will never outweigh the risks of ditching meat and other animal products. Also, never forget that any new food in a dog's diet should be introduced gradually.

Rocky loved treats, and I gave him many, many more than I should have. I often didn't read the labels on them. I didn't look at the price tag either. I just chose whatever he liked. I thought that was perfectly fine. Now, I wouldn't recommend doing this for anyone. But do your own research, and use credible sources to find out what works best for your pet. For instance, you can start by finding what meat by-products are legally permissible in pet food. And please do yourself a favor and go with your gut when making decisions for your companion. Also, please don't wait to take action into your own hands when your companion gets sick because—if you are like me—you will be in a panic and won't be able to think rationally. Even if you are entirely different from me, always remember that some diseases progress fast, giving you very little time to do anything to help your beloved.

Traditional medicine still views cancer as a death sentence. Conventional medicine will treat symptoms rather than the root of the problem. Some medical practitioners don't believe certain foods, supplements, medications, environments, and mental states can lead to cancer, even though they can. Again, do your research. Some pets go into remission without conventional treatment and stay there for many years. Some people combine conventional and holistic approaches for their furry family members. Some furry patients live long lives and pass from natural and not cancer-related causes.

With a solid wish to help Rocky feel better, I kept looking for new treatments and reaching for new hopes. My research led me to products made in countries that ban genetically modified food or have it under strict regulations. As a result, I started ordering supplements from New Zealand and Australia.

Be aware! Regardless of their qualifications, some veterinarians are too quick to recommend euthanasia. For example, if your vet is not a radiologist, how certain is he or she that your pet has cancer just by looking at X-rays? Pet doctors are only human and can make mistakes. Also, some of them are more experienced and compassionate than others. Choose one wisely!

Trust your intuition. Months before Rocky was diagnosed, every dog that stopped on the street to exchange some sniffing with him had an expression on their face that deep under my skin made me feel so uneasy. But I brushed it off. Studies show that dogs can smell cancer, and cancer definitely stinks in every way possible. I thought about that each time I saw an alarming look on a dog's face, but I tried to convince myself nothing was wrong with Rocky. *I am blessed with a healthy dog. Dogs develop all kinds of diseases, but* not my Rocky. It would never happen to him. There isn't any unbalance inside of my pup's body. I tried to believe in that. Not long after that, Rocky's fur, especially around his belly area, developed a specific odor, one that was hard to describe and even harder not to notice. I took him to the clinic, where he was diagnosed with a yeast infection. He also received his yearly shots (shots should be avoided in animals with any health condition). During the visit, I brought a little cyst near Rocky's belly to the vet's attention, but she assured me it was just a fat mass that would go away on its own. I didn't request further testing. I was even in a hurry to leave the vet's office that day and rejoice that my boy was still strong at almost thirteen. But deep inside, I knew something was wrong.

Cancer hurts. Cancer is physically and emotionally painful, even though your vet might have told you your pet is not in pain. Know this before the pain becomes too hard to bear; sooner or later, it will, especially when the body is close to losing the fight. Remember, nobody knows your dog better than you do. Once you know what kind of disease you are dealing with, try to calm yourself as best as possible, as everything you do, say, or think can affect your pet. Many of us, at some point in our life, will know or come across someone with cancer. It is important to acknowledge here that one size doesn't fit all. If no physical pain is involved, emotional pain is present. Always. A dying body's pain is real. The pain of saying goodbye can't be measured. Dogs are very good at hiding both.

If you are going to give CBD (Cannabidiol) oil with over three percent of THC (Tetrahydrocannabinol), always ask for a lab test of the product. Ensure the oil has the expiration date printed on the bottle and has not expired. You will find many people online selling these oils with a high price tag and claiming promising results. However, many of those people don't care at all about the well-being of your furry family member. Also, they know the law is still more on the side of people than animals.

Watch out for the dosage they recommend. If they keep telling you to increase it, as they instructed me, that is a red flag. Their primary goal might be their profit. If you choose this option, keep in mind that even if cannabis is legal in your state or country, this treatment method is usually not prescribed or recommended by many vets. But what would a person not do for those they love? I personally didn't think twice about anything that could help Rocky feel better and prolong his life.

Familiarize yourself with cancer in animals even though your pet is healthy. If you are unfortunate, like myself and millions of other pet lovers, to watch your furry baby suffer from it, I promise you there will not be enough time. Cancer acts fast. Sometimes veterinary patients have months and sometimes only days to live by the time it is diagnosed (remember, they are more skilled than people at hiding their discomforts). There are numerous cancer-causing chemicals our pets may get exposed to—everyday products like home cleaners (especially those that contain benzene), scents, pesticides, grooming products, water and food bowls made of plastic (yes, BPA is harmful to dogs too), water from creeks and lakes, and the list goes on. Also, if you are concerned about chemicals that can be found in your tap water and you filter it before use, do the same for your pet. Some of the chemicals, such as mercury and lead, are associated with severe illnesses, including cancer. According to the National Cancer Institute, every year six million dog cancer diagnoses are made. Cancer is the leading cause of death in dogs, and one in four dogs will die from it. Lymphoma is among the most common cancers in dogs, and dogs are five times more likely than people to be affected.

Our pets absorb our energy and emotions like sponges. Just like children, they are deeply affected by your attitude and actions. If you want a healthy and happy pet, live a healthy and happy life. Of course, none of us knows when and how we will die, but we should take control of all that we can control. I could still see

Rocky's blue eyes shining and his helicopter-rotor-like tail speeding each time I got up from my chair and reached for a leash. But I could also still feel the warmth of his coat when he was lying next to me, trying to cheer me up when I was hurting.

Find peace in yourself first if you want to transmit it. If you are not at peace, you can't do anything properly. Even loving someone will not come easily to you. If you are not at peace, everyone, especially animals who are more sensitive than people, can feel that and be negatively affected by it. If you don't practice self-love, you will give yourself and others much less than you and they deserve. Remember, not everyone takes time and energy to learn to be at peace. It might be too late if you wait to change when hard times come. Is that what you want?

Take some time to take care of yourself. If you put yourself in last place, even if you continue to function, you will never do it properly. Self-love is not selfish, it's necessary. Lack of self-love and care can lead to unhappiness and disease. And your pet will follow you because you are the leader of the pack. Your pet will mirror your condition and do everything to help you find the right way, the way to yourself. They will do anything to help you realize that life is a gift that should be appreciated and cherished.

Just like children, our pets need us. But when children get older, they become less dependent on us. When pets get older, they need us more. Their short lives are happy when they can rely on someone who knows the joy of living and the joy of loving.

Last but not least, regardless of the outcome, remember, cancer never wins. Cancer has nothing on the love your dog has in his heart, and such love thrives beyond the physical body. Cancer will never know love because it can't be just or merciful. So why have any hate for it? It deserves nothing but pity. Cancer cannot break ties between you and your companion. Cancer will lose its battle with love. Always. No exceptions.

After Rocky's body became still, while caressing his fur, I

touched his neck where minutes ago his lymph nodes had been so enlarged that he could barely breathe. There was no longer any sign of them having been enlarged. At that moment, I knew that the cancer had died. It was erased like some tiny, insignificant dirt under the raindrops. But my dog was still there. His silky ears felt the same when my lips touched them. His paw was still warm, and I could hold it in my hands for a long time for the first time in my life (Rocky was always too sensitive for paw touching). As never before, I felt the warmth filling my heart, and I knew he was resting inside it, breathing peacefully. I didn't want to wake him up.

If you have ever loved a pet, you know how much that furry baby brought comfort and happiness into your life. They do anything to make you feel accepted, appreciated, and loved. If you are miserable, sick, or depressed, there is no way your companion will feel good, healthy, and peaceful. After a while, they will mimic you and become everything you are. They become your identity that nobody can steal from you. Especially not cancer. They go everywhere you go. You never get separated. *Never*.

But again, go with your gut feeling. I only provide my suggestions and share my experience. To tell you what your dog needs wouldn't be right or fair. Every dog is different, and every human companion they share their life with is different as well. I have seen dogs never getting one shot in their life and eating only leftovers but living a happy, long life.

I have also seen dogs being pampered and fed food made with ingredients some humans can only dream about, but they don't even make it to their adult years. Doesn't this happen to people too? We simply don't live alone in this world and can't control the cleanliness of our drinking water, the health of our food, the safety of the products we use, and the honesty of the people we put our trust in. Then nature plays its role of being angry at those who destroy it and punishing us all in one way or another. When taking a dog into your home, you do your best. Sometimes things work the way you planned; sometimes, they don't.

One thing is certain: your pet depends on you. Your pet can't make choices for themselves but does have hopes for the best life with you. Whatever you do, look into their eyes and remember that even your mirror shows you your inverted image, but your pet's eyes reflect your actual image, your true self.

In my journey through soul- and self-discovery I met some wonderful people, and they pointed out where my path could take me. All of them came and left. All of them had a lesson for me that I needed at that particular time, and then they moved on to teach someone else. Ultimately, I realized all I need is to open my heart, forget about the brief encounters, the temporary items I have, and the temporary body I am living in, and reach out to the leader of my angel team to guide me. To feel peace, to be free, and to enter the beautiful space the universe has reserved just for me, I just need to call Rocky.

Chapter Twenty
BOND

Nothing in the universe is created faster than the bond between a child who struggles to find a friend and a dog with eyes begging for love.

Even on my busiest days, I found time to watch and enjoy interactions between Rocky and Zorel, especially when she was a toddler. There was so much simplicity in all the activities those two engaged in—playing, relaxing, and communicating in their unique ways. Sometimes Zorel would tell him—or I should say, ordered—what character he would be in her imaginary game, and he would comply. It didn't matter to Rocky if that meant wearing silly hats, police uniforms, sweaters, or princess crowns. He took on each role as if taking his favorite treat. Then they would switch their roles. Rocky would stretch out and walk across the room toward his water bowl, and she would follow him. On all fours, they remained on the same path with the same dedication—like a lily pad and a frog, together they continued with the flow—Zorel and her dog.

So many times, I wished to join their play. Sometimes I did. But I never stayed in it for long. I always occupied my mind with emails that needed to be answered, school papers that needed to be graded, assignments that needed to be completed, and bills that needed to be paid. Today, I would give anything to see all the members of my favorite pack together again. Getting down on all fours would be fun. Showing them that I prioritize love would be a choice I would be proud of.

I believe we all come here to learn. Our mission in life is complete when we learn what we need to know. I am sure Rocky learned how imperfect humans are. His own human was a great example of that imperfection. He still gave his love with no judgment to everyone, but especially to Zorel and me. We loved him the best we could. We would never stop.

For the past few years, I spent a substantial amount of time cross-posting about shelter animals daily. Social media channels or group administrators often blocked me for exceeding the number of daily posts allowed. But I did what I felt I had to for the sake of those who don't have a voice to speak for themselves. These dogs were strays or owner-surrendered dogs. About ninety-nine percent of the time they were big dogs. Most were malnourished and scared with the saddest looks in their eyes.

While some people discard their pets, others would do anything to make their furry family members live healthier, happier, and longer lives. Some people foster and rescue dogs nobody else wants, including the old, blind, and tripawds, just to name a few. This gives me hope, hope that a dog or any animal that is given a second chance at life can open a person's heart. Maybe slowly, because some people may not be very teachable. Yet surely, because everything is teachable. From my experience, nobody can love more and soothe pain better than dogs.

How come more people don't give dogs a chance? Why are so many "humanely euthanized" every day rather than adopted? Puppies. Beautiful dogs. Playful dogs. Loving dogs. Lack of space? Lack of funding? Lack of time? It doesn't matter because people will always find some excuse for shutting doors to love. After all, throughout our lives, many may offer us the key to a healthier, happier, and more content life, but if our "door" is closed from the inside, even with the right key, nobody will be able to get in.

In 1999, Catholic Charities was my sponsor for immigrating to the United States. In the summer of 2019, while working as an ESL instructor, I passed by one of their offices every day on my way to school. Soon I learned about their children's story time and reading program for new immigrants and saw that as an opportunity to show my appreciation to this organization for helping me. I decided to become a volunteer.

Upon contacting the program coordinator and expressing my desire to join their team, along with my therapy dog Rocky, she told me something I had heard a million times before. *Not all cultures and religions have positive views on dogs. Not everyone wants to be around them. You can't bring your dog.*

On that day, as on many days before, I wished people could see Rocky and Zorel interacting with each other. I wished they could see it the same way I did. There is no more incredible bond formed; there is no more important lesson learned. Love is all they know. Love is something all of us should know.

Chapter Twenty-One
FAITH

It is amazing to know that no matter where you go, how far and for how long, there is always someone waiting for you.

To believe in something means to be connected to it by love, reciprocated love. If you love someone without input from them, that's not belief or faithful love, and it rarely grows into something beautiful. Sharing beliefs connects people more than sharing lifestyles, beds, food, and interests. Trusting someone who believes in you is the highest form of love. Being fortunate enough to find someone who can help you find faith in yourself is the best benefit from friendship you can have in life. I assume that not being judged by what you do but instead by being appreciated for who you are, happens only to those who are chosen. I am glad that Rocky chose me.

If you hold any religious belief, you will get many opportunities to sit next to people who look and behave differently from you. Some will sing into your face. Some will wear their lipstick from ear to ear. Some will talk and talk and always have more to say. Still, you will feel connected to them because they worship the same deity as you. If nothing else, you may feel more comfortable around them than around people in the fifteen-items-or-less-only register line who are giving you angry looks for having sixteen items in your cart.

At first, I didn't share Rocky's belief in unconditional love. I was leaning more toward a selfish kind of love. He didn't seem to mind and sacrificed himself to show me what I was missing in my life. I was too busy to notice. That is, until his soul freed itself from the physical world.

When I realized I couldn't connect with him, not because his body was no longer moving but because of my lack of belief, I was devastated. I was lost because I chose to travel in the wrong direction. I used my free will not so wisely and remained on the same path, reaching the same destination. Pain. More pain. Always pain.

All his earthly life, Rocky was trying to teach me that if I believed in him as he believed in me, we would never be apart. For example, during our last night together, he could breathe peacefully only when I held his head in my hands and spoke to him: "It's okay, it's okay." He knew it was okay to leave because he felt connected to me, no matter where he was. But foolish me would beg him to stay because I was afraid that everything would be gone when he closed his eyes, and I would have to face the world without him. As much as he loved me, I had no faith that what is created in true love stays there, whole, as love is.

In life, second chances are rare; in love, there is always room for them. But they must be earned. I am showing Rocky that I am on my way to opening my heart and keeping it that way. Now it's time to see him with my heart only. To embrace him with it. I believe in my capability to do so. I can feel his presence and the strength and courage it gives me to live in the moment. Most of all, I believe that his love is the light I see every day when I open my eyes and the light I will go to when I don't open them again. Yesterday we walked next to each other. Today I am following him so we can continue walking together tomorrow.

I knew I would need some time to put my thoughts down and write this book, but I believed with my whole heart that I could do it. What I didn't know was that I would ditch my two PhD degrees in progress (one of them ABD—all but dissertation) and begin studying Reiki, animal communication, and grief counseling. I didn't know whether my anger at God for taking Rocky away from me would ever subside or disappear. I couldn't even imagine that my most challenging time would make me a more humble, understanding human being. I was unaware that I was becoming grateful for the limited time in one life and limitless time in another. I couldn't imagine that my soul could ever hang out somewhere between Heaven and Earth, traveling through a beautiful astral plane and faithfully waiting for Rocky to come back to me, come back to us, come back home.

All begins with pain, with suffering. Life itself. Faith too. This is because, especially in the beginning, everything is uncertain, but uncertainty leads to a heart full of fear instead of a heart full of wonder. Then suffering becomes a reality, a daily routine, a habit that's hard to break. But grief is something else. It is a chance one must take to become a small, almost invisible particle in the universe. From there, one can continue being that small or change and grow. Hitting rocks doesn't come with instructions. It can't be learned from books or movies. It must be first-hand experience. It must create a deep wound in the heart that nobody can cure. Healing is possible only if you allow yourself to be shaken to the core.

I wake up every day knowing Rocky's sacrifice wasn't and couldn't be all in vain. It instilled in me a thirst for learning and finding more than I could see and reach. It also proved to me that some people are born to connect with one animal more than they could connect with the entire human population. Because that animal understands them better than anyone else. Loves them more. That animal reflects the life they want to live and the mark they wish to leave upon the world. The animal is always there to guide and love them and help build their faith. We have to open our hearts wide enough to hear them when they speak to us and believe in their words. Only their messages have meaning that can make one's heart sing each time it is ready to cry.

A dog living in spirit knows those they left on Earth still experience life through their limited senses. After all, a living force once occupied their body that we could see, touch, and feel next to us. Communication with them doesn't cease once they enter a different form of life. It continues. It happens every day. Simple things like song lyrics on the radio, billboard signs, or the chatter of people passing by. I discovered that even in my most profound sorrow (especially then), I need to observe what is happening around me. I mustn't forget that despite the pain, I can take a new breath and release the old one. I can find new pathways spread around old roads. I know this. This is a choice I make every day. It is my belief. It is my response to Rocky's love.

Sometimes it feels like I am putting together the pieces of a jigsaw puzzle when I am trying to find the true meaning of words I hear, actions I witness, and people I come across. Other times, everything is crystal clear. That, however, doesn't mean the spirit of my loved one is not willing to engage in clear and concise communication with me or refusing to connect. This only indicates that my heart is occupied with something else—heavy emotions such as worry, stress, or anger. In such situations, the heart keeps its door ajar or completely shut rather than wide open.

Some animal psychics believe pets may come back to us when we ask them to. But they emphasize that a lesson must be learned for them and us upon their return. There is also no guarantee of "happily ever after." Even though I don't want Rocky to experience the suffering surrounding this world again, I will be ready to listen and understand him better. I will be prepared to show him how far I've come. I will be prepared to be a better me, for him and everyone around me. I want my Rocky back.

When I think of his return, I always imagine a dog crossing my path while I am behind the wheel. I stop, and as soon as I step out of my car, I know it is Rocky. He lifts his head and runs into my open arms. That was what happened on July 5, 2021, though not in the same way as I pictured it. A black dog was on the opposite side of the road, eating something from a little box. I made a U-turn to get to him, pulled over, grabbed one of Rocky's leashes from the passenger seat, and opened the door. I tried to examine my feelings as I approached him. I felt no connection with the dog. I was cautious; I was getting closer to a stray animal, which is not necessarily a good idea. He was big. He was eating. He seemed unaware that I was coming. He may have been abused and terrified of people. Maybe territorial. He might act out of fear and attack. But I was determined to get him off the street.

I was about six feet away from him when I noticed a young woman running toward us with a leash in her hand. "Is this your dog?" I asked when she crossed the street. She confirmed with a smile. The dog lifted his head for the first time, and our eyes met. I was amazed by the shiny black fur on his face and a bell-shaped white spot around his neck. He was stunning.

After the girl had him on a leash, he pulled her toward me and landed a couple of warm kisses on my hands. Then he gave me a big-doggie smile. I smiled back. I knew that wasn't Rocky's soul in a new body, but it felt good. It was like an introduction to the story that was starting soon. It was like Rocky borrowed his body to tell me he was on his way home. Animal communicators call this a "walk in," but for me, that was just a beautiful sign from Heaven.

I know Rocky will be with me to cheer me on and love me no matter what and no matter where he is. Once you love a dog, don't fear walking a lonely path, because you will always have him by your side. Now I know that because I feel Rocky's presence everywhere I go.

Chapter Twenty-Two
I DIDN'T LET HIM GO, I SET HIM FREE

Love can't be owned, only shared from one heart to another.

Since that horrible morning on November 10, I've been waiting for signs and dreams where I can see his beautiful eyes again. I want to touch him and feel his presence. But nothing is happening. Everything is so awfully static. The weight of the silence is so heavy to carry. Emptiness follows me everywhere. There is no escape. Not even an allusion to peace.

I started meditating. I've never liked dealing with my racing thoughts, as they often crash my attempts at mindfulness, but now I feel I have to face them. When I close my eyes, I see only darkness and only feel the impact of my mind that bumps into me, bringing anything but calmness. I'm not spared from this pain. Not even for a second. How could I be?

I keep trying to meditate. I try to calm my mind. I talk to it because I can't talk to people. They don't hear me how I want to be heard when I talk about Rocky. They don't understand that some grief takes a long time to move to the acceptance stage. But what should I accept anyway? That Rocky is far from sight but not from the heart? In a better place now? Waiting for me at the Rainbow Bridge? I am not too fond of any hearsay that gains popularity in hospitals, funeral homes, social media, etcetera, etcetera. I dislike formality. People sometimes use words and phrases only because they assume this or that is the right thing to say. Then they move on to another bereaved person, another tiding of bad news. There is always something to talk about and very seldom something to be compassionate about.

I keep trying to meditate and find a connection with Rocky. I want to hear from him about life on the other side. Where is he? How is he? I want to hear from my boy. I just need to see his eyes, to get closer to the answers. But no message is coming through.

Some time ago, while trying to meditate and connect with Rocky, I said, "Rocky, tell me where you are." In my mind, I heard this: "Neither on Earth nor Heaven." That's when I knew I needed to do something to help him. I needed to show him and myself that I was no longer in control and couldn't change anything that had already happened, except letting my pain go between Rocky and me . . . between Rocky and Heaven.

A few days later, I found peace in silence and signs of light in the darkness during another attempt to meditate. This gave me confidence and motivation to keep trying. From five-minute meditation, I moved to half-an-hour meditation. Now it was hard to open my eyes because I knew I would have to leave that comfort behind. And for the first time in a long time, I felt Rocky was still that tiny puppy who needed me. And no matter how hard he tried to use all he had to talk to me, I couldn't understand all he was saying. When the right time comes, I will. He waits. We both wait.

During one of my afternoon meditations, I asked Rocky for a sign of whether or not I should study Animal Reiki. Ambulance sirens announced themselves right away. That was my answer. I knew I should dive into learning. Two days after that, I closed my eyes, imagining angels taking Rocky to the place they call Heaven. I didn't want him to be stuck between Earth and Heaven anymore. I could feel that being earthbound was painful for him. My furry child waited for my blessing to be free to fly, and I gave it to him. I didn't cry. I smiled for him and his joy. I felt the peace he was surrounded with in my heart. I smiled for both of us.

I asked Rocky again where he was at that moment. A car drove through my neighborhood. The music from its radio played loud the Tom Petty song "Free Fallin'." I opened my eyes and grabbed my phone, eager to find and read the lyrics.

My best friend never promised something he wasn't capable of doing. Now his soul is no longer imprisoned in his body. If I could look into Rocky's eyes right now, I would be able to read many wise and kind words in them. I imagine him running through the fields without a leash, as he always liked to. No people around to complain. No dogs barking at him in disapproval. He is free now. I couldn't let him go while he was on Earth, but I set him free now. Differently from Petty's song, my Rocky is free, free flying. If he ever falls from above, it would be right into my arms.

> Run, run, my boy.
> I set you free,
> To be happy,
> To be at peace,
>
> Run, run, my boy.
> But when our paths cross,
> Never forget me.

FLY

I held a bird
I was showing her to all
As a bride her ring
I held a bird
And danced through life
She loved, she could
Beautifully sing

I held a bird
I was showing her to all
As sunlight its ray
I held a bird
And dreamed through reality
She loved, she could
Come to stay

I held a bird
I wanted to stretch a moment
To forever

ROCKY

I held a bird
I didn't want to cry
But I did
Heavens called her to fly
I didn't want to speak
But I did
One last dance,
One last kiss,
And
Goodbye

Chapter Twenty-Three
ENERGY AROUND US

I feel like a mountain when my dog looks up to me.

If the numbers on your electric bill are the first thing that comes to your mind when someone mentions the high price we pay for energy, think again. The following scenario may give you food for thought. It is Wednesday morning. You wake up with a smile on your face. You have many things to smile about: refreshed mind and a well-rested, pain-free body; beautiful dreams from last night; happy birds chirping merrily nearby; the child still sleeping; room enough so you can stretch in your own bed; no work to do for hours; thoughts not racing—not yet.

The day progresses similarly. You enjoy everything: food, weather, even "catch me if you can" and "teach me if you can" games your child invented just for you. Then you decide to take your little one to the playground. There you run into a parent you have met before. Their child and your child like to play together. The other day, you learned that you have some things in common with this person. The children can play, and the adults can have some adult talk. Pretty good. However, this parent, this mom, her day hasn't been as good as yours. She doesn't smile much normally. Today, she doesn't smile at all; she is having a bad day. And before she tells you about all those things that went wrong for her, you feel like a squirrel looking for a hollow tree to hide in from a predator. Unfortunately, you cannot escape, and her low-frequency energy overshadows all the good things that happened to you. An hour later, you drag your tired body back home, and this time, your negative thoughts are eager to show you how fast they can race inside of your head. You are miserable. So miserable.

This happened to me, and I am sure many people have experienced something similar. Yes, I dragged myself back home, but thanks to my guardian angel Rocky, who is always there for me and who always operates on love only, I could access high-frequency energy soon. I felt the embrace of peace again.

In a world packed with bad news, bad vibes, and poor connections, everyone will need help at one time or another. People invest a great amount of time and money in finding solutions to improve one's life. Yet one complex thing doesn't have to lead to another. The substance of a joyful life is simplicity. By following the path of love, one can see beyond the clothes people wear or the frowns they share. When nothing seems to work, to a heart that knows love, peace is more accessible. One simple loving thought can create ripples of positive energy. I can still see Rocky's eyes every time he moved closer and waited for me to pet him. He knew no matter how under the weather I felt, with him next to me, the sun would shine again soon. He still does that. I can feel his soft fur when he is nearby.

I ignored the importance of energy, even though deep inside my heart I knew that energy is everything and we are all energy. After pleading to God every single day to help Rocky find his way back to me, at least in my dreams, and getting no response, I became silent, distant, and mired in my pain. I looked for the slightest sign but got nothing. I often closed my eyes, wishing never to see the light again. I didn't expect that silence and darkness would not only make my pain more bearable but also lead me to the realm of peace and light that I had never experienced before.

As I started peeling off layers of ignorance based on my attachment to the physical world, sparkles of hope started appearing around me, calming me, and even bringing joy. I finally acknowledged the presence and importance of my spiritual sense. This brought back some moments when my godsent angel, Rocky, tried to communicate with me, like on the day when Zorel and I drove to downtown Houston with a grasshopper on the top of the hood. The ride took about forty minutes at over sixty-five miles per hour, but our unusual passenger never left his spot. When we reached our destination, finding a parking spot took me a while, so I forgot to check if that little guy was still there. When we returned to the car, he was gone, but I still smiled while thinking about that visit even hours later.

Or that day when Zorel and I walked in the park where the three of us used to go for picnics. As we approached the tree Rocky loved to relax under, we noticed its trunk appeared different; it was so colorful. When we moved closer, we saw beautiful butterflies resting there. There were at least fifty of them. No exaggeration. No imagination. Just life in its purest form.

On Sunday, January 17, 2021, Zorel and I took thirteen balloons to a nearby park. We wrote our "happy birthday" messages for Rocky on them and started looking around for a good spot to release them. Although this was the busiest day of the week for this very dog-friendly park, only two dogs crossed our path. One was an adorable German shepherd puppy, and another a beautiful, full-grown husky. They both resembled Rocky.

Months after Rocky's transition, Post Malone's song "Circles (Let It Go)" often played on the radio, and every time I heard it, my eyes filled with tears. But due to the song's popularity, I soon forgot about these "coincidences." After that morning when I watched my precious boy lying on the sofa and leaving this world—the world I couldn't imagine being lively and beautiful without him—I often forgot that life still continues.

More than half a year later, I can't even recall how many times I turned my car radio on to Michael Jackson's song "You Are Not Alone" or Rod Stewart's song "Have I Told You Lately That I Love You?" They started playing when I drove around places that brought up many happy memories of Rocky.

My favorite meditation moments are when I feel Rocky's fur on my face and arms. Every time I meditate on my bed with my legs under my comforter, I feel his paws nearby. I know it is him because Rocky always moved around very carefully when he was in bed. He made sure never to step on me, no matter what position I was lying in. I knew it was him. I feel that he never left. I know he always sleeps next to me or somewhere in the house. This time, we are even more connected because this is a heart-to-heart connection where all senses become one. All of them are love.

Have you ever been in the same room with someone or sitting close to them but felt alone? Or even worse, sleeping next to someone but felt like you were surrounded by ice-cold water? Or feeling so uneasy whenever a family member even mentions they will visit you? These are all examples of what is inside us, what matters, and forms a connection—a deep and unbreakable connection. Our perception doesn't form according to the outer layers of a person, even though we often rely on first impressions or assumptions. It is not regulated by the DNA we share. This is energy. If we trust our gut instincts, such trust can lead us to the right decisions and relationships, those that last and those that make us happy.

My experience taught me to believe that if you have someone who is no longer present in your physical world, you can still be connected to them—sometimes even more than to anyone else. It also taught me that the more dependent I am on the physical world, the more I am disconnected from that of the spirit. Regardless of your experience, take a moment to step inside your inner world and just breathe. And whatever brings a smile to your face, believe in that. I believe God sent me Rocky because he knew I always longed for a family but never had one. I believe Rocky was my angel from day one. He guided me through life. He still guides me.

The other day I sat in my chair while my daughter played with her dolls on the floor. In the middle of her playing, she lifted her head, looked at me, and said, "I know you're thinking about Rocky right now."

Speechless and motionless, I just stared at her. "How do you know this?" I asked after a few seconds.

"You smile, Mom. A lot," she answered, beaming. "Also, yesterday when you took your nap, you had a dream of him. You smiled the same way."

I couldn't find any words. I didn't even try to. A single tear fell down my face.

But more followed when she added, "While you were dreaming, you were moving your hand. I think you were petting him. You also said something I couldn't understand. Maybe I love you . . . or something like that."

In my first book, *Born in Sarajevo*, published more than a decade before I even knew the universal energy called Reiki existed, I described my belief in good and bad energy. I still believe that destructive energy surrounding people who committed crimes against people and humanity—those who committed mass killings in wars, for example—can't be destroyed by imprisoning them or taking their lives. It takes lack of followers and, ultimately, lack of belief to destroy it.

I witnessed that in the aftermath in my country. This country is no longer war-devastated but remains spirit-devastated because repairing buildings is much easier than repairing broken souls. And I know broken souls are attracted to negativity, as I was one of them. If a person didn't change while living in the human body, they wouldn't change in spirit form either. A new life form doesn't bring new energy; they belong to the same heart. And a heart is either closed or open. An open heart means connecting; a closed heart means cutting ties. An open heart can give and receive love; a closed heart can't. While one couldn't imagine what going through their life with eyes closed would be like, they may not think that having a closed heart is something to worry about. Not until they are lost. Not until they hurt. Only you can seek the way to open your heart, and your life is your opportunity to do so. Do it right now. Tomorrow might be too late. Don't procrastinate. Love. Simple as that.

Dogs are born with their hearts open. We humans must learn how to open ours. We must be willing to do so. We must be willing and keen to remind ourselves daily that our hearts need to be open to love. Not having the willingness is common for us.

The other day, I was in the car with my daughter, driving on a highway, when a truck with a long trailer drove past us. The trailer was full of cows. Their bodies were pressed against one another, probably preventing them from taking a full breath. Their heads were lowered. I could only imagine their sadness and pain. Upon seeing them, Zorel exclaimed, "Look, Mom, cows!"

Being one of those parents who tries not to sugarcoat anything, I said, "They will become food, not pets."

My daughter instantly became silent, staring out the window. A few moments later, I heard her crying. While trying to direct her thoughts toward a happier subject, I realized that children share animals' sensitivity to the world around them more than we grownups do. Although I don't eat meat from animals that live on land (occasional seafood is my guilty pleasure), and I was saddened

by what I had seen, I didn't cry. How many adults would? With our heads buried in pains from the past and worries about the future, many of us are ignorant about life and living right now. If we were not, we, and all living creatures we share this planet with, might live happier lives. We would enjoy our presence in this world much more. We would be like children and animals, free to have fun without trying to gain anything or striving for perfection. Being free to just be.

TODAY I WAS IN A HURRY

Today I was in a hurry.
I couldn't wait to come back home
To come back to you
As always, I missed your company
People scare me sometimes
People are too demanding sometimes
So many questions to answer
So much time to get wasted
Waiting on busy phone lines
Waiting in stores,
Waiting on streets
Waiting to catch my breath
Waiting to live
So many red lights
Even more red faces
So many 'press one for English' prompts
Meaningless words, words that hurt
Shouts that are unnecessary
I was in a hurry to escape the world

People and emotions
Spinning in the circle
And come to you
Kneel next to your paw
Then let you lead me
Wherever you take me
Let you show a safe touch of love and
Let me taste the sweetness of peace
One short walk
Always brought me a long-desired joy
Your flapping ears made me smile
Your sticking-out tongue made me laugh
Your blue eyes made me feel as if I was
Swimming in calm waters
I was in a hurry
To open the door
Step in
And see you waiting for me
But when I did,
The icy walls and empty space
killed my
Excitements, my hopes,
My dream
Tomorrow, I would
Be in a hurry again
This silly heart can't unlearn that
Every day starts and finishes
With you

I KNOW YOU KNOW

Today is one of those days
When I can see nothing but a huge
Hole in my heart
It feels so fresh
Like the bullet just
Rushed through in and out
Letting it bleed
Drop by drop
Until none is left
I avoid everything that
I loved once
Singing of birds
Scent of flowers
Rainfalls reaching the arms of the lakeside
I avoid everything
Because everything reminds me of you
Not being here
I know you may not understand,
It may surprise you that I can't feel you

Being next to me
I know you know that you never left my side
You also know that every night I close my eyes and wait to see you
And every morning, I open my eyes and wish for the same
Until then, I would keep avoiding everything
That reminds me of you being so close but so far
From everything we shared together
Everything that was ours

Chapter Twenty-Four
REIKI

There is a lot one can learn about patience by looking at a dog's eyes when he wants something.

I am a huge skeptic. That's probably written on my forehead, and I am not ashamed of it. I'm not afraid to question information and experience to find the truth. I've studied criminal justice for many years, and there is a good reason why hearsay is not admissible in court. I believe it shouldn't be acceptable in everyday life either. My philosophy is if I didn't see it, don't expect me to believe it. But do I believe a hundred percent in something I see? Not necessarily, as I know what we see can be very deceiving. For instance, differently from hearsay evidence, eyewitness testimony is admissible in court, and it is often enough to convict someone. Yet eyewitness testimony depends on a person's memory that can be "polluted." Thus, eyewitness testimonies can lead to errors; errors can lead to costly loss.

I think belief goes way beyond all senses and emotions. For me, to believe in something or someone means more than loving them. I have love for many people, but I would never put my trust in them. I know how toxic they are for me, yet I would never turn my back on them. I also know that certain foods are bad for me (my sweet tooth is my number one enemy), but I would probably never stop eating them. I feel joy when I buy and consume them, and I am never angry at them for hurting my body. I use my free will when I allow them to damage my health. This short-lived happiness has long-term consequences, but it satisfies my need for instant gratification without representing my deep, heart-felt belief.

That said, when I have faith in something, love is always present and always different than love held where there isn't faith. It is stronger. It is reciprocated. But before I am involved faithfully, I selfishly and stubbornly wait to feel love and faith coming my way first. That's what happened when Reiki found me.

The first question people ask is "What's that?" Before answering, I smile as I remember asking that same question myself. We are all different, so I never try or expect one answer to fit all, but I can share one that suits me. I always believed in energy and did not doubt that everything is energy, so for me, any form and phase of life is a new form and new stage of energy. Every time we make any movement, physical with the body or mental with thought, we create energy, and energy creates us. We produce many different energies, and many different energies make us. Finding our purpose is finding the energy that stands out for us, the one we are meant to cherish and protect but are not afraid to spread out. Until we realize this, we will never know about our ability to connect to the universe. When we do, we connect to the substance of life, which is belief, and to the source of life, which is love. That's what Reiki is for me—faith in good energy, faith in love.

The first time I came across Reiki was weeks after Rocky was diagnosed with cancer. A member of one of the many Facebook groups dedicated to dog cancer I joined offered so-called distance animal Reiki for free. Because I was late to join this Reiki group session, I decided to at least read the comments. I was surprised (remember, I am a huge skeptic) that every single person claimed they and their pets were very relaxed after the session. Many people attended and they posted close to one hundred comments. Since I was willing to try anything to help Rocky, I wasn't happy about missing that opportunity. But I put little thought into this and soon forgot about it.

Six months after Rocky's transition, I found a book that touched on this subject. I was taken aback because I picked a book that was a dog story (*Tyson's Gift* by Brandon Wainwright) and didn't expect to find anything about Reiki there. I didn't realize that universal life-force energy is indeed about dogs. Dogs know a lot more about energy than we do. They know that energy heals anyone—people and animals in any space, at any time. They also know where the energy is needed the most and where it can bring the highest good.

Now not a day goes by without me learning something new about Reiki. Each time I do, I have a stronger desire for knowledge. I am drawn to Animal Reiki and believe I am called to practice it. But for now, I do self-Reiki only. Although I can't wait to start working with shelter animals, there is plenty of work I need to complete in my inner world first. I still need help from universal energy to clear and balance energy points called chakras in my body before becoming a solid channel for helping others and the animal world.

The reason I believe we are all in need of Animal Reiki is that we still don't appreciate what animals do for us. They love us even when we feel unlovable and save us from our own and other people's judgment.

Animal Reiki focuses not only on an animal but their human companion as well. One can't help them if they don't know how to help themselves. Only God knows how miserable I was for years and how much that affected Rocky. God also knows that nobody but Rocky was there for me, trying to ease my pain and put my broken soul back together. Everything could have been much different if I had known about energy healing then.

Animal Reiki is also essential because professionals like trauma therapists and grief counselors are not trained to deal with the trauma of pet loss. From my personal experience, some of them are far from being animal lovers, and they would harshly judge you for giving such importance to an animal's life. This can provide you with two options. Either you can bury your pain deep inside and become afraid to show it or help yourself and others like you. I tried them both, but I stuck with the latter choice.

The humbleness, honesty, and compassion associated with Reiki practice fascinates me. Reiki is based on five principles: just for today, do not anger; just for today, do not worry; just for today, be honest; just for today, be humble; just for today, be compassionate. Many Reiki practitioners I came across don't refer to themselves as healers. They describe the entire process as *opening channels for the healing energy coming from the universe.* This means that one doesn't have to possess a special gift; instead, simply turning toward that energy with an open mind and heart is enough. Again, we are all part of energy. We are all connected. For some, that may be a hard pill to swallow, so they let their ego rule that out. But some view this connection as an opportunity to learn from each other and grow.

Dogs, and animals in general, can teach us so much about life, as their love differs from that of humans. Their love doesn't come with expectations. They love selflessly. They don't need fancy words to show their love. Animals touch your heart in a way nobody else can. They do so by embracing energy that connects them to others. They are not puppets on a string, as people often treat them. They are true leaders, true healers.

What I've learned so far is that Reiki healing is not about a wish that will come true, but it is about knowing that whatever happens, it will be for the highest good. Embrace it. Healing starts with being on the right path. Sometimes that path leads to the body's freedom from physical pain. Other times, it leads to the soul's freedom from the physical body. Months ago, love energy might not have given Rocky more time on Earth, but it might have given him peace when he needed it the most. But I didn't know how to receive it; unconsciously, my heart was blocking it. Energy flow is my and Rocky's peace now. I am peaceful because I am connected to him. Rocky is peaceful because I finally opened my heart and have faith in love, faith in the never-ending story of life.

    I will do whatever it takes to learn where Rocky is and if he is okay. That comes as naturally to me as the air I breathe to stay alive. I keep my hopes high and my skepticism at bay. For the first time in my life, I fight nothing. I go with the flow. I miss my boy so much and wish I could turn back time to find a way to heal him, hug him longer, and see him standing beside me wherever I go. What I know, however, is that guilt and grief block me. They don't allow me to dream of Rocky, to receive signs from him, and to feel his presence. I also found that Reiki serves as a cleaner for any of my blockages. Reiki is a cleaner of my space.

    When I had my first Reiki session, I had no expectations and tried my best to relax on the massage table and not let my mind follow my racing thoughts. As the music played in the background, I found it soothing, especially the sound of ocean waves. This brought back memories of Rocky—happy memories. I heard his bark. I envisioned him herding Zorel in when she swam out too far. Yet, no matter how much I tried to visualize him looking at me, I couldn't. He was too far, seemingly unaware of my presence. Fog surrounded him. Every time that fog started disappearing, his image was under its veil again. I was squeezing my eyes closed, pushing tears back. I was pushing my arms and entire body harder against the table because I was tempted to get up and run, trying to reach for him.

    The session ended. Someone tapped my shoulder, but I didn't

move. I laid on my stomach, my head buried in the table's face port. I dared to open my eyes when I got myself in a sitting position. The stream of tears took over.

The Reiki practitioner handed me a box of tissues without saying anything. I kept my head turned away from her. I dealt with my pain alone, as I was used to. It took me some time to stand up from the table and take a couple of steps toward a chair in front of me. Before sitting down, I turned around, and our eyes met. "Are you okay?" she asked. I nodded slowly, still crying.

Her following statement made me almost stumble and fall on the floor. "You had a pet."

I just looked at her for some time and held my breath. "How did you know that?" I finally asked.

"I always ask a guardian angel of the client to take the lead of the session," she said, adding with a warm smile on her face, "Your pet did that."

"My dog. My . . ." —I even surprised myself by choosing not to disclose Rocky's name— ". . . my everything." *This is too personal,* I thought, glancing at the woman. Too precious to me to share with anyone. Especially someone I just met.

"Your dog wants you to know that he is okay. He's glad you're here, connecting with him. Also, he wants you to get another dog," she said, pausing for a second before adding, "When you are ready, of course."

I looked at her without blinking, making no sound. My heart was bleeding. There was no way she could know about Rocky. At the beginning of the session, I only mentioned that I had been grieving and that my heart chakra was probably blocked. I never said anything about my dog, my Rocky. How could she know this? My inner voice kept questioning. I started shaking. My tears couldn't stop falling. I silently called, "Rocky, Rocky."

A sudden thought popped into my head. He really wanted me to know about Reiki. He wanted me to heal. It occurred to me that she and I were not alone in the room. My guardian angel was certainly there too. My angel. My Rocky. I looked around, feeling a warm smile landing on my face and drying my tears.

"What are your thoughts on reincarnation?" I asked.

"It can happen," she said without hesitation.

My smile reflected my inward joy. "I believe he is coming back to me."

"Maybe . . . when you're ready?"

"Yes."

On my way back home, I had mixed feelings. One above others —*Rocky is trying to set me free*. That made sense. That was what he spent all his life doing: making me happy. Rocky knew that when I was with him, I was joyful, and I was always myself, never pretending to be somebody else or trying to live my life according to other people's expectations. I indeed loved many dogs, some of them mine, some of them not. Like many other dog lovers, it's also true that I had a special dog who was half of me. The better part, for sure. My soul dog. That dog was him.

How could I ever imagine another dog in my house? Was it even possible to kiss some other dog, think about Rocky, and be happy simultaneously? Did he really want me to do that, or was there something more to it? For those of you who have experienced the joy of a true love but were forced to go your separate ways, you will know what I am talking about. Yes, it does make sense they want you to be happy, but it also makes sense to you not to be able to even imagine happiness without them.

The higher power is the higher power. But it should be about keeping together, not dividing. Now, I may analyze too much. But I have to know what my dog is communicating with me. Nothing is more important to me than that. When a soul becomes one with the higher power, as Rocky did, I must stop and listen. All I can think of is him. I don't want another dog. I don't and can't have another soul dog. I only want Rocky. All I can hope for is that one who believes in a higher power, such as myself, can reach it with an open heart. People say your belief will define your life. And I believe Rocky will share another earthly life with me.

"Only when you are ready to have another dog," the practitioner said as if reading my thoughts. "You are not ready yet." She warmly smiled again. "You will know when you are."

I will be ready when Rocky's good old soul enters a new living body, when my boy is ready to return. "That's right," I said.

As I think of everything he taught me and live my life according to, he keeps sending me people and circumstances that are adding something new and better to my old self. With each new sign, he proves that I am on the right path. He patiently waits for me. He reminds me that I still have time. He sends me what I need to keep going. If not, why would a family member who denied my existence keep trying to get in touch with me after Rocky entered the spirit world? This helped me find the path of forgiveness. Why would Zorel meet many children at a playground whose parents became my friends? I didn't want to engage in conversations. I wasn't open to friendships. But interestingly, most of those people broke the ice with one word: dogs. This helped me find an occasional way out of the long, lonely road I was on. Why would they, of all people, choose me? This helped me find my hope path. As I become more connected to the world I live in, more doors open that lead to my guardian angel. And I can't describe how hard it is for me to do that in the surroundings I desperately tried to fit in but never could. How hard is it to get out of my skin while changing my old habits while I grow?

After my Reiki experience, as before it, I didn't know what my life had in store for me or when and how it would reach its final earthly point. But I knew that with a guardian angel like Rocky, there was nothing I needed to be afraid of. There was nothing to be scared of since May 17, 2008, when he chose among almost seven billion other humans, to love me. Rocky always found the perfect place and time to be with me. He still does. I look forward to being at those places and sharing those times with him. My past and future with Rocky are now. I remember what we had and occasionally can taste what is yet to come. And that's enough. More than enough.

I don't think Rocky would ever be aware of or even ready to admit what he had and keeps doing for me. He was always too humble to show the world that so much beauty would be impossible to shine without him. I was a lost soul when he found me. Not anymore. Regardless of where life takes me, I know I will find peace by listening to my breathing, happiness by appreciating my life on Earth, and love by following signs from Heaven.

Why did Rocky want me to practice Reiki? Why would a skeptic like myself want to hear about the power of something I can't see? Why would someone who hasn't known about warm touch since birth believe in "healing touch?" Why would a chronic victim ever want to learn about healing anyway? These were some of the questions I tried to answer. The purpose of Reiki answered all of them. Treating heartache is not as powerful as treating what caused it. Causes are many. Causes are deep. Causes don't disappear with a magic pill. Causes mean working on yourself, not on others. Causes mean there are battalions of effects coming to destroy you. You can't remove the enemies all at once, but you can get rid of them one at a time. You can avoid dealing with many effects when resolving the one cause that created them. Because of Rocky's love, I started searching for causes inside myself to save my life, to save my child's life, and to bring him back.

Rocky showed me the five precepts of Reiki before I even knew Reiki existed.

Do not anger

I never, ever saw—even once—Rocky becoming angry. Yes, he

had dislikes, but he shook his disapproval off. The world's negativities tried to affect him, but they seemed to only pass through him, never causing him to be unforgiving like me.

Do not worry

Every time I was about to leave Rocky and travel back to my European home, I saw the worry in his eyes. But this was more of a loving attachment he had with me than a not-living-in-the-moment-based worrying. I was the one with my head buried in the past and my feet stuck in the future. Rocky didn't worry when his favorite dog park was full of aggressive humans and their pets who followed their "master's" behavior. He knew there was always another park. He didn't worry when we had no car and had to walk everywhere. He enjoyed that we were together. He didn't worry when we found out he had less than two months to live. Rocky was just sad because he knew I was too preoccupied with his condition and would miss seeing that he was still there, still my best friend who loved me.

Be honest

Rocky didn't think about honesty; honesty was part of each of his breaths. When he put his head in my lap, he was honest. When he looked into my eyes, he was honest. When he proudly walked next to me, he was honest. When he was happy to see me when I returned home, he was honest. Rocky spoke with his heart, and his heart was always open.

Be humble

During his earthly life, Rocky made me believe that I was the one who rescued him. He wanted to make me feel like I was the best friend, parent, and person to be around. But *he* was the one teaching *me* about friendship, who was parenting me and making me smile. He never took credit for helping me stay alive and teaching me how to live.

Be compassionate

Sitting in schools and libraries next to children who struggled to read and listening without judgment was Rocky's way of building communities filled with young minds that believe in themselves. Rocky's source of happiness was making others happy. Rocky's source of love was his love for others.

In the summer of 2021, Rocky led me to Shelter Animal Reiki Association (SARA) and its founder, Kathleen Prasad. Only a few months later, I became her student for Animal Reiki. My life will never be the same. With Rocky's guidance, it gets better every day.

Chapter Twenty-Five
ANIMAL COMMUNICATION

How to live in the present moment: spend more time with dogs than people.

Do you think that communication felt by the heart is more meaningful than anything that can be put into words? I believed that Rocky understood all my emotions, actions, and thoughts. He listened to them when nobody else wanted to. He responded by staying by my side when I didn't believe I was worthy, cheering me up when I was down, and sharing my joy when I believed I was reaching the sky.

When I started learning about Reiki, something else came into the picture. The subject of animal communication caught my attention months after I'd received my first messages from the other side from Rocky. That was, in fact, a warning sign. During a big winter storm in Texas in February 2021, I was visiting Dallas and decided to take a risk and drive back to Houston. We had a short break from the rain and snow on that particular afternoon (Wednesday, February 17). The temperature dropped below twenty degrees, and thick ice covered the roads. But I was determined to drive back home. Or at least try.

At ten miles per hour, it would take me a long time to reach my destination. As I was approaching the highway, I started feeling an uneasy sensation all over my body. Instinctively, I glanced toward the dashboard display. It read: Die. What I found interesting was that this word was on display even after the music ended. I thought about Rocky while giving a left-turn signal and making the U-turn. I knew that while nobody else cared about us, my angel did. I started looking for a hotel for Zorel and me. Rocky wanted us to be warm and safe. He wanted us to stay alive.

During my years with Rocky, I learned I am far from being a good relationship buddy. I like to have the last word. I want to be in control. When I sense I am losing control, I usually respond with anger. I become angry at myself, people, and God. Angry at everyone and everything.

When I found out, as veterinarians predicted, that I had only two more months with Rocky, I felt imprisoned. For those of you who have a control freak in you or have ever dealt with one, know that we try to go full speed without stopping, even when stuck on a dead-end street. We can keep hitting the wall, refusing to acknowledge its strength. When that happens, a person is unable to be true to themselves and others for a very long time. Even when the pain breaks us down, we act like conquerors, like winners. I was about to learn that I could fool the rest of the world, as my thoughts and feelings can be hidden deep inside, but I couldn't fool my dog. Ever.

Rocky knew my parents were not involved in my life. I had no loving adult relationships. Surrounded by strictly enforced rules, I used anger as a survival tool. When he came along, he didn't judge me for that. What I didn't know—or maybe I was afraid to admit—was that every time I hurt inside, he was hurting too, but since it is well-known that dogs are more sensitive than people, that meant he was hurting more. I believe that until he was able to resist the pressure of the pain, it didn't affect him much physically, mentally, and spiritually. His shining light of love could dissolve even the greatest distress. But even super dogs like him lose their superpowers and realize it is time for their human to pick up the broken pieces of themselves and learn to be responsible, wise, and strong. Even angels like Rocky start falling when they give their wings to those they love more than life.

When Rocky became sick, I tried to pray, but my heart was not open enough for my words to reach as far as they needed to. Once again, I felt like a failure. Then I returned to my comfort zone. I dedicated most of my time to being angry and weak. I couldn't function properly. I couldn't help myself or the one who needed my help the most—my precious Rocky. I watched his suffering but didn't end his pain. I prolonged it. I scheduled euthanasia many times but canceled it at the last moment. Instead, I asked and pleaded with Rocky to stay with me. But when I realized his body was no longer on a cancer roller coaster—one day promising, another day devastating—and it was just going downhill, the control freak in me was wide awake and asking for the torment to end. My anger demanded an end. My weakness begged for an end. Then my guilt started swallowing me piece by piece when the end finally came.

Carrying Rocky in my arms became my reality. He disliked that, but he wanted me to believe I was helping him. He let me take the wheel on each of our final rides. Like all the other rides we went on before. He was the only one who put up with all the weaknesses that came in a package called me. He knew there was so much strength I never reached for.

As I am writing this, seven long months have passed since I held my beautiful puppy in my arms. Time has come not to disconnect my behavior from the damages it caused. I will never be perfect, but I can omit many errors in my life. For example, I can get rid of that control freak governing my life and let the energy of the universe heal me and lead me. Rocky is a big part of its light now. I can feel safe. I can put my trust in it.

In one of my recent meditations, I asked the energy (without trying to influence it in any way) where Rocky was. As in every other spiritual practice, growth happens when layers peel off slowly, one by one. In my experience, one of those layers led me to a door. Then I was entering one long hallway after another—some of them full of lights, some much darker. The last hallway led me to an image of glittering sunlight on water. I didn't see Rocky in it, but I felt his presence. I knew I had the answer to my question because I knew how much Rocky loved to swim. I smiled because I knew my baby boy was happy where he was, and he wanted me to be happy here. I can only make this come true by learning to understand animals, as Rocky understood me—mind-to-mind and heart-to-heart. No words are needed. Rocky was born with that gift. I am just learning about it now.

I know Reiki and animal communication found me because Rocky showed the universe that I was ready to learn. He was the only one who truly understood why the road to my heart is so rocky—my Rocky. My Rocky, wherever he is, has faith in me, as he knows I can do more in my life. I can become a better person from the one he remembers.

After extensive research, I found Karen Anderson, an animal communicator specializing in afterlife animal communication (Karen is also the founder of the Painted Rain Ranch animal sanctuary), and enrolled in her course. Led by my guardian angel Rocky, I gained confidence in communicating with the amazing animal kingdom. Every day there is something new to learn.

For my internship, I had several connections with pets using a photo where I was required to ask them specific questions (written by the instructor) such as who is their favorite person or guardian;

their favorite food or toy; their likes and dislikes; and so on. The following is one of them:

Milo (name changed because I believe we should protect pets' privacy as that of humans) wanted me to know that no matter where he is and what he does, he always finds time to enjoy peace and sunlight. Especially when he is surrounded by a lot of colors. The background in this picture perfectly describes Milo's choice of surroundings, as well as the joy he has inside himself. He also loves toys that are very colorful. He prefers orange because it represents his softness and warmth and red because it represents the love in his heart. Milo prefers to be in a relaxing mode rather than a playful one. He is a wise guy who likes to "preach" to those in need.

Instructor's feedback: "This sounds just like Milo! He is a very mellow boy and has low energy. He is very wise, all knowing, and has high vibrational energy. He loves his spots in the sun and is surrounded by beautiful flowers and plants in the yard outside the windows. He has an orange toy that is his favorite of all! Great job! He is an exceptional soccer player and will bring the red ball to you to play with him. Wonderful! You did so well with Milo. You should feel very proud of your abilities!"

As with everything else, I needed more proof that what I was getting was not just coincidental. So I buried my head in books, enrolled in courses with different teachers, and volunteered my readings to any animal lover who was open to them. I connected to cats, dogs, rodents, horses, birds, and fish; living, missing, and those in the afterlife. Some of my animal communication practices were more successful than others, but one was exceptionally unusual.

On April 13, 2021, I came across a post on social media. A woman was pleading for confirmation that her soul dog, who crossed the Rainbow Bridge two months earlier, visited during her session with a professional animal communicator and shared his messages. According to this sweet lady, many of these messages "did not really resonate" with her. She only wanted to know that the dog, who had been her little angel on Earth, was still watching over her from Heaven.

Since I am passionate about connecting with dogs in spirit, I decided to volunteer my efforts and time to respond to her post. On that very day, I tried and I tried, but nothing happened. I truly wanted to be able to tell her at least something, yet I kept sitting in my chair with my eyes closed without feeling any energy from her boy. Just silence and my thoughts which included: *Thank God this is not a live session so you don't have to embarrass yourself.* After twenty minutes, I gave up, opened my eyes, and got ready to stand up. At that moment, I noticed something had fallen from one of the kitchen shelves. I stood up, walked to it, and picked it up. It was a little blue pen. I didn't think anything of it, but when I turned around and headed to my room, another object fell, this time from a table right in front of me. It was my daughter's blue stuffed toy. Right away, I knew what to do.

This is part of the message I sent to the woman:

He felt loved, appreciated, and connected. He still does. Color blue is very meaningful to him. Perhaps his favorite toy?

This wasn't the first time pets communicated with me through colors. And this wasn't the first time somebody told me my message made them smile and made their heart sing with joy. In this case, the reason was a blue toy. As the woman said, "A blue fetching ball with rope was my dog's favorite toy." This was also not the first or the last time I would get proof that nothing but love can reach beyond time and space. When we let love take the lead, we will always find a way.

Chapter Twenty-Six
AFTERLIFE

People leave dogs behind for many reasons; dogs always find a reason to stay.

What you will read next is not research-based or part of oral tradition—stories passed from generation to generation. It is something that happened to me. Because these stories are very personal, it took me some time to decide whether I was going to "expose" them. When it comes to Rocky, I'm very selfish. But I know Rocky would not mind sharing them. I believe he would support me and be proud of the person I have become. *Love is life; life is love. Love never dies.* This is how Rocky lived his life and wanted me to live mine too.

If you need a research-based book on the afterlife, I recommend *Evidence of Animal Afterlife* by Edward Anderson. If you are interested in learning about mediums and their interactions with those in spirit, you may want to read *The Medium Explosion: A Guide to Navigating the World of Those Who Claim to Communicate with The Dead* by Robert Ginsberg. There are definitely other good books that resonate with me, but these were some of the first I read in the early stages of my grief. As in my previous chapters, I recommend you do your homework, find your own answers, and always remember to go with your gut. Not everyone can be on the same page, as there are many pages in the book called *life*.

This subject may be touchy for many, but once again, I am sharing my personal experience with the afterlife. It all started on July 10, 2012 when I witnessed my grandmother taking her last breath. As I mentioned earlier, my grandmother was my only parent, sibling, and friend for many years. She was the only human who ever cared about me as a child; she was my everything. Seeing all that gone in one second devastated every petty part of myself. I screamed for help and begged the paramedics to help her as they entered our apartment only a few moments later. One of them yelled at me to stop and let them do their job. I covered my mouth while tears streamed down my face and just watched. I wasn't prepared to lose her. I wasn't ready to let her go. I wanted them to bring her back, believing they could, not knowing it wasn't up to them. It wasn't up to Earth but up to Heaven.

After about twenty minutes, they retrieved her pulse. The ambulance took us to the hospital, where two hours later, her heart stopped. What followed in the next few hours and days was something I had never experienced before. Many colors appeared in my dream on that very first night. Bright colors, beautiful colors, colors I had never seen before; they appeared before my eyes, but I could also feel them around my entire body. They were warm and uplifting. Messages started coming in.

As described in the chapter titled "Dream Child," my grandmother wrote and visually described that I was going to give birth to a girl named after her. That I was going to publish a big pile of books. That I couldn't follow her because I hadn't completed my mission on Earth.

I woke up and noticed something unusual about the chandelier above my head; its electrical ceiling box was detached, and the light's fixture wires were loose. Later that day, lights went off entire apartment. No rain or any adverse weather conditions ca that. I knew it was my grandmother telling me she was still around, still with me.

I took my grandmother's ashes to her hometown of Sarajevo, where they were buried in a family graveyard next to her mom and brother. I have stayed in our apartment in Sarajevo many times since then. Each time when I was there, she gave me a sign that she was nearby. On one night while I was in bed sleeping next to my daughter, the radio turned on by itself and started playing the song I remembered from my childhood: "*You live in clouds, little girl . . .*"

I got up, turned the radio off, and went to check on Zorel. She didn't move and continued to sleep soundly. I, on the other hand, couldn't go back to sleep. Yet I closed my eyes, dedicating all my thoughts to my grandmother. Not long after that, I felt warm breath touching my face, and then soft lips landed on my forehead. Just like my grandmother used to do. Just like when I was a child. Her favorite spot to kiss. A single tear rolled down my face, but I kept my eyes closed. I smiled. "*Baba*, I love you."

My grandmother loved and was very proud of her hometown. Even though many of her family members lost their lives there during World War II and decades later she was forced out of her home, mistreated, and almost killed during the civil war. Until her last day, she never stopped talking about Sarajevo. It didn't surprise me that she was back home. This time, she was happy and free of people's prejudice, free of her worn-out body, and free to walk the streets she knew so well.

In one of my first dreams of Rocky after his transition, we were together, doing something we both loved: riding in a car. What surprised me the most in that dream was that I was in Sarajevo with Rocky. I always wished to bring him there during his time on Earth, but I never wanted to put his life at risk. Hearing all those horror stories about what happened to pets in a plane's cargo section scared me so much. I didn't want him to get injured from objects and suitcases falling on his crate, feel anxious from turbulence and earsplitting noise from a plane engine, or die from dehydration, heat stroke, or heart failure. I didn't want him to be stuck in a crate alone and afraid for over twenty hours. Besides, I knew how stressful loud noises and thunderstorms were for him. Not until months later, I realized Rocky took me back to Sarajevo because he wanted to show me he was there with Grandma, waiting for me.

Like Grandma, Rocky loved his hometown. Zorel and I took him to Dallas when we received his ashes. When we reached the halfway point of our trip from Houston, the radio started playing Ozzy Osbourne's song "Mama, I'm Coming Home." I glanced at the little box in the passenger seat and touched it gently. My eyes were filled with tears, but I smiled. "Yes, you are," I whispered. "You are coming home."

The next day after Zorel and I finished shopping at the grocery store, we returned to the car to find one of its windows rolled down. "Look, Mom," Zorel said, pointing at it. "We didn't leave it this way." It was the left one, where Rocky used to stick his head out and where he liked to entertain every pedestrian and every car passenger he saw by sticking his tongue out.

In another dream, I was standing in my kitchen when the lights went off. My legs were positioned in a weird, zigzag way. Something warm and furry filled the empty spot between them. I knew it was Rocky. As much as I longed to turn the lights back on, I didn't want to move or scare him off. So I reached down, and my hand landed on his back, right next to his tail. I stroked him. I knew he was afraid of something I wasn't aware of, as he always stayed close to my legs when he felt that way. His entire back felt tense under my hand, but slowly he relaxed. Soon, I couldn't touch him anymore. I was no longer in my kitchen either. I was at a river or lake where Zorel was swimming and diving (more diving than swimming, as she usually does). She disappeared and didn't come back to the surface. I waited a few seconds, assuming she was trying to prank me, as she had done many times before, but she was still under the water. I tensed up, just like Rocky did earlier. *That's it, I've waited long enough.* I jumped in the water, trying to find her, but I felt like I was swimming under ice and getting swallowed by darkness. I finally found her. She was lying at the bottom of the lake. She didn't move. I wrapped one of my arms around her and used the other to swim to the surface. I carried her out and began CPR immediately. Nothing changed. I kept trying. Her cheeks started inflating like two little balloons. She was about to spit up a great deal of water. But before she did, I woke up and went straight to her room. I held my breath until I saw her breathing. She was very much alive but deep in her own dream.

At that time, I was still unaware that Rocky had tried to pass a message on to me—a warning, to be more precise. He wanted to prepare me for what was about to happen. Indeed, two days later, we were in an emergency room because a little part of a toy Zorel was playing with got stuck in her nose. It took an hour for a doctor to remove it.

August 10, 2021 marked nine years, one month since Grandma became a spirit, and nine months since Rocky joined her. It was also a Tuesday, like on July 10, 2012, and November 10, 2020. Months earlier, I had a dream about this day. I had seen a neighbor from my childhood who passed away long ago. She told me that on this date, I would visit Heaven, or Heaven would visit me.

I sat there then and thought, *If this is my last day, I will never be able to see my child being independent and grown up. Whatever it is, Rocky is there for her and me. We are family. In whatever realm, we will find our way to each other. That's what family is for. Traditional or not. We have each other's backs. We love one another.*

ROCKY

On August 10, I indeed had a visitation from Heaven. While I was charging my cellphone, the power adapter produced a radio static sound effect. As I tried to push it deeper inside the electric outlet, the sound stopped for about five seconds but then returned.

The following day, I had a confirmation that my visitor from Heaven was there to stay. At noon, while I was on the phone, I received a notification that another caller was trying to get hold of me. The number on my caller ID was 0000000000. According to many books I've read, zero represents infinity, divinity, and angels. It proves that Rocky still lives and will continue his life journey, regardless of time and space.

Later that day, I came across the street dog I tried to catch and, if nothing else, help find a safe place and loving family for. Her face had scars; her eyes were full of sadness and fear. It appeared she recently had puppies. While trying to give her some water and leash her, I sat down in the grass, looked at her, and asked, "Are you Rocky's soul? Are you my boy?" The dog wasn't interested much in me, and when she found out that I had only water and no food, she turned around and walked away. But even before she did, I knew my heart would know Rocky in any shape and any form of life; my heart would react differently if that was him. Still, I wanted to help the dog, so I followed.

I called her one more time with the hope that she might come back. To my surprise, she did. This time she kept more distance between us, looking at me and waiting to see what I would do next. I didn't like that I had nothing more to offer her except a bowl of water. I could tell she was about to leave again. She gave me one last glance, but instead of walking away, she took a few moments to do something that brought a smile to my face. She started rolling in the grass in the same way Rocky did. By witnessing her sudden happiness, I saw Rocky's spirit showing me he is always joyful and ready to send me a sign of his love for me.

When she disappeared from my view, I went back to my car

and followed her. She led me to her pack. There were five or six more dogs, from a ten-pound dog to an eighty-pound one. Some of them were on a leash and some were running loose. They all barked at me. But she stood in front of them. Her chest appeared broader as she held her head high while looking me straight in the eye. She was fearless, indicating that I was dealing with the leader. She started circling my car, as if telling me, "It's time for you to leave; this is not your territory."

Many people I know have had at least one session with a medium to find out what happened to their loved one after transitioning to the "other side." Many of them hit their lowest lows before seeking help. Some of them unfortunately ended up with "professionals" who charged them thousands of dollars per session. But they felt lost and desperately needed to get back on track.

I considered that path for some time, but I chose another one. I never found a medium to connect with Rocky because I didn't want anyone else to communicate with him. Nobody except myself. It was too personal. I was too selfish. I didn't want to let anyone in. I didn't want anyone to see my pain. Most importantly, I believed Rocky wanted something else, something more. So instead of crying all day, feeling sorry for myself, and feeling guilty for not being able to save Rocky, I started learning. That was how I began putting myself together. But not the old pieces. I started building a new me. Before I knew it, lessons began unfolding before me.

What I've learned is that mediumship, even though it revolves around "talking with the dead," is not about some innate talent or superpower; instead, it is about channeling a connection with the spirit. I believed that I could become such a channel with Rocky's guidance and that the heart-to-heart relationship Rocky taught me would be my vehicle for learning the language of the spirit. My only purpose was to get closer to him. Through all dimensions, frequencies, and bridges, I wanted to reach my dog and touch him as he touched me in this life. I tried to silence the loud noise of ego and feel that peace that only Rocky could give me.

My learning consisted of reading books, watching educational videos, taking classes, and practicing. I wasn't even a bit surprised when I learned that even though I occasionally experienced *clairaudience* (clear hearing), *clairolfactance* (clear smelling), and *clairgustance* (clear tasting), *clairsentience* (clear feeling), *claircognizance* (clear knowing), and *clairvoyance* (clear seeing) are my dominant senses. Just as I could feel that Rocky was very uncomfortable deep inside, even though he acted the same on that day when I took him to the vet and found out he had cancer. Just as I could feel him walking on my bed when his physical body was no longer in my view. Just as I could see Rocky's body covered in a white sheet and being carried away from my home by an unknown man weeks before I knew the way it all would end.

Some mediums claim that living beings are made of eighty percent spirit and twenty percent physical existence. Many of us will never become aware of that. Thus, we will never reach a higher vibration during our time on Earth. Occasionally we might feel it, but we will not understand it unless it becomes a daily part of our lives.

When I was six or seven years old, I had a dream that a distant relative died. I woke up late that Sunday, just before noon. I slowly entered our kitchen where my grandmother sat and sipped her coffee. I wasn't sure how to tell her about my dream or how she would react. I just felt the urge to share it with her. "Grandmother, I want—" Knocking on the door came faster than the rest of my words. Grandmother's sister-in-law was at the door. As soon as she stepped in, she said her mother had passed away the night before. I nodded, glancing at them in total silence. I was glad they didn't notice my reaction because I couldn't wait to walk away and forget about everything.

I wasn't a medium then, as I am not a medium now, but I know and learned from those who believe that such a possibility is open to all of us. It all depends on if we take it and work on developing it or just dismiss and turn away from it. Since Rocky left a significant hole in my heart, I opened myself to all the wonders of the universe. The most fascinating for me is the energy that changes forms but never ceases to exist. Once I develop more of my clairvoyance, or clear seeing, I believe I will be able to see Rocky again in some new form, but with the same good old love he has for me.

Lately, dreams don't come easily to me. It is like a heavy curtain is now between them and me. I ask for them. I am waiting for them. I hope for them. Still nothing. When I close my eyes, it seems that I am doing a favor to my body and mind and giving them time to rest. But I let my soul starve, and I don't know how to help it.

One day I took a brief nap before leaving to pick Zorel up from school. I didn't expect to find myself in a nightmare. People chased me, and I tried my best to run away from them. I kept glancing behind me but couldn't see anyone. I only heard them as they galloped toward me. *I'll not let them catch me. I'll not let them get me.* I believed I could escape. But then I found myself in a place where I could barely move my arms and my legs. It felt like a cage. I was caught. That was it. The end. With eyes wide-open, I swallowed my fear-filled screams.

"It's my grandma," I burst out.

"Tell me about your grandma." I heard a woman's voice but couldn't see what she looked like. I could feel that she was standing nearby, but a heavy fog prevented me from seeing anything.

"It's my grandma," I repeated. "My angel."

"I love you," the voice said. "Until you're gone."

I opened my eyes, left with mixed feelings and many questions.

Was that Grandma? If so, what was she trying to tell me? Did it have anything to do with Rocky? What did "I love you until you're gone" mean? *I love you, and I'm with you until your last day on Earth? Until we see each other again?*

I could feel my grandma everywhere in the room, and I knew she was standing close to me. Reaching for my face and hands. Smiling. I didn't know at the time that she had come to tell me something very important. That message was her and Rocky's gift to me. I'll share that gift with you in this book's last chapter.

BOND

Like two lighthouses your eyes are shining
They are a key
That unlocks the heaviest doors;
You always waited
Beautiful and elegant
On all fours

You still wait
Only this time you stand before me
With your golden wings;
A melody of your happy *Ah-roo*
Carrying my soul high to show me
Love continues to live with little, magical things

Chapter Twenty-Seven
LETTERS

Once you fall in love with a dog, your life will never be the same; it is always better, richer, and more content.

After seeing her and Rocky's book, *Rocky and a Girl with a Curl,* on a library shelf, Zorel asked, "Is this book still going to be here after we die?" I nodded with a smile, placing my hand on her shoulder. "Of course. Love always lives." She looked at me with her eyes widening with excitement. "Like forever?" I nodded again. "Forever."

With a big grin on her face, she turned to the first page and read, "For the magic or dreams." Then she flipped to the author's notes at the end. "Many years ago, I listened quietly as my grandmother read a story to me. It was about an adventurous hero and a beautiful princess. As I heard the story, I imagined that one day, I would find my hero and princess. My dream came true. On May 17, 2008, a furry hero named Rocky came into my life. And six years later, on May 17, 2014, a princess, the girl with a curl, entered my world. Yes, dreams can and will come true . . ."

"Saturday is my favorite day," I said to her. "May 17, 2008 and May 17, 2014 were both Saturdays."

These following letters are a combination of the dreams and hopes of a little, untraditional family. Zorel. Rocky. And me—Mom. Writing helps us with our grief. Whatever you want to say to your loved one but can't anymore, remember, you can always write to them. Your letters may help you with your grief. They may bring back some old sweet memories and make new hopes sparkle. They can remind you that a heart-to-heart connection never faces a closed door. With that connection, everything is open to love; it's never too late for love because love knows no time, distance, or borders. It's never too late for a new beginning. It's never too late to reach out one more time for the one you miss. It's never too late to discover your own version of forever.

I started writing these letters in my phone's notes app. I just kept writing with only Rocky on my mind. I had no idea these letters were my first steps to creating this book. I had no idea that I would write a book ever again. My grief was overwhelming. I was in survival mode. I was trying to keep moving and functioning, not because I wanted to stay on Earth, but because my child needed me.

I began reaching out to Rocky to find a light in the tunnel. I needed to talk to him, to tell him I believed he was forever alive in some wonderful and just world. I needed to show him I could do more than just sit with his pictures in my arms and cry. With this belief, I could do much, much more.

Dear Zorel,
    The following letters were written to me by you and your mom, but I don't remember you sending them. I found it inter-

esting that dogs don't receive letters in Heaven. Dogs don't receive letters on Earth either. Dogs don't receive letters, period. Yet that doesn't mean we don't read them. It doesn't mean we don't understand them. It doesn't mean we are not sitting next to you and feeling joyful and proud while watching you write them. And certainly, it doesn't mean we can't respond to them. Especially when they come from hearts we are connected to. In Heaven. On Earth. Wherever we go. One of these days, I'll come to you in your dream, and we will sit next to each other, as we did so many times before, and read them together. As always, you are going to ask me so many questions. I don't mind. I can't wait to hear everything you store under those pretty curls. I can't wait. I can't wait.

Your big four-legged brother, Rocky

April 22, 2021

May 17 will always have a special place in my heart. On that day, in 2008, you came into my life. On that day, in 2014, your sister Zorel was born. We are only days away from that day, and I'm sure this year will be the happiest one yet. I'm sure the three of us will celebrate this day together. I know you will be back. But let me tell you something. Although I loved you dearly and tried to make your life the happiest I could, I carry a heavy burden of guilt.

I genuinely believe that my life, which revolved around a "sorry circle," made you so unwell. I was constantly sorry for myself for being surrounded by people who hurt me and sorry for hurting people myself. I was unforgiving, angry, and ignorant. I didn't deserve someone like you—so good, precious, and pure.

After your lymphoma and liver cancer diagnosis, I selfishly kept you alive by feeding you food you didn't want to eat and giving you the medicine you didn't want to take. You were in and out of the emergency room in your last days, and I kept scheduling and canceling euthanasia. I wish somebody else had been there to make that decision for me. This was an immense weight to bear. I wasn't strong enough. Your passing was not peaceful, which hurts me more than words can describe. I can still see, hear, and feel your struggles to breathe.

People abused my trust when I was seeking help for you. They met my expectations—a lack of compassion was present in their words and actions. Because COVID-19 guidelines didn't allow me to accompany you into doctors' offices, I had to sit in my car and wait for hours for someone to call me and tell me you were still alive. During those visits, you often received treatments I didn't agree to and medication that weakened your already-weak body.

I prayed for cancer to leave your body. I didn't hate it. I tried to fight it with love. It didn't work. In the end, I begged God to share this merciless disease between us so you could live longer. I wanted more time with you so badly. That didn't work either.

I can tell you I am not a firm believer in "they are in a better place now" or "Heaven gained another angel." I also don't want to wait until I cross the Rainbow Bridge to be with you again. I know this life and world are far from perfect, but they are all I have for now. And you are the one who taught me to live now and enjoy every moment. I have faith in angels and know how much this world needs them (certainly more than Heaven does). You are my angel. You are your little sister's angel. She's waiting for you. She knows you are coming back. The other day she told me, "Rocky came into my dream." She paused, taking a long moment to read the sadness on my face. Then she added, "He will come into your dream too, but you have to become a better person, Mom. Jesus loves you. God loves you. You know that being sad and angry is not good for you." I nodded, trying to hide my tears, but they choked me piece by piece. "Don't give up, Mom, never give up."

I moved the curls away from her face with one hand and wiped my tears with the other one. I looked into her big brown eyes. I didn't know where all that wisdom came from. She is not growing up in a religious home. We don't discuss the Bible, Quran, Torah, or any other holy book in our house. Where did all that come from? Where?

Then I got it. I came across one book after another that shed light on my child's message: have a religion or no religion at all, but you need love and forgiveness. They both come from your higher self. Leave your heart's door open. Embracing this imperfect world with all your imperfections is not your weakness but your greatest strength. Yes, sometimes a few simple words from a child can give your life a whole new meaning. Sometimes her simple words are all you, my sweet Rocky, and I need. Sometimes she doesn't need to say anything at all for me to know that you loved us more than life itself.

Something else also came to my mind. I have come across many devoted believers who told me all about sacrifice "Jesus did for his people, people of the world." Their eyes lit up with love and passion as they narrated story after story. Right now, I may face backlash from some of them, but I will say what I have to say. I don't seek understanding anyway, as I experienced my childhood and adult traumas without anyone's desire to understand or help. And many of them were caused by men. Some considered themselves nonreligious, and some were all about their religion. All of them preached about what I should and shouldn't do, and all sentenced me to distinction. So how could I believe that any man who walked on this Earth could sacrifice his happiness for mine or give his life so I could live? Only you, Rocky, sacrificed everything for me, Zorel, our little family, our little world. You did that without hesitation, with love, and selflessly.

Yes, I questioned God, I cried to God, and I was devastated. I was angry. Guilty. Confused. Rigid. Numb. Dissociated. Completely dead inside. I didn't understand why God took you, especially in such a painful way. You, of all beings I have ever met in this life, didn't deserve that one little bit.

What I didn't know then was that I sought God. More than ever, I connected to God with pure faith. I didn't realize I was truly becoming alive in those moments when I felt more dead than ever. I didn't know God would bring you back. God knew; his love for you was already prepared for your—our—next life together. God showed me through you that when my faith in what I don't see is strong, when my faith is deep, darkness becomes light, sadness becomes joy, death is temporary, and life is forever. Now I should never question the perfection of goodness, and I should never doubt the presence of goodness. And I should never think of myself as not being worthy of being part of that goodness. God showed me what true love is through your sacrifice. There are no limitations, no false assumptions in that love. God also showed me that this Earth is and will continue to be, as one of my old textbooks reads, "a beautiful rocky planet."

Because God couldn't show me through people I came across in my life, God showed me what faith is through you. He showed me what it looks like when a sinless being walks the Earth and shows you that his love for you is more significant than anything else. That sinless being will forgive you all your wrongdoings, put you on a new path, and transform your life forever. When the right time comes, I believe —my faith tells me that you are coming back to me. Love without faith is delusion, not love. Nothing is more truthful in my life than this love I feel for you.

God knows that trauma, especially childhood trauma, is not

easy, if possible, to overcome, and in every inch of my being, I carry their burden. He knew my response to trauma was dissociation. From the cradle, I dissociated from all the beauty found in life, love, and faith. One of the marks I live with is a lack of trust in people. And God knew that as well. He also knew I had a hard time talking to him because he is portrayed as an omnipotent man, and, as I mentioned earlier, every man in my life, sooner or later, expressed a desire to overpower, control, and abuse me. Many succeeded in one way or another. He knew all I needed in my life was you. All I needed was faithful, nonjudgmental love to be saved. All I needed was love that the rest of the world could call whatever it wanted, but I would cherish everything about it. No need for traditions. No need for one-size-fits-all. No need to divide he from she, the two-legged from the four-legged. No reason not to call love faith and faith love. No reason not to have a belief that fits who I am rather than who I am expected to be. What true believer would even try to be something they are not and turn their back on something so sacred to them if someone disagreed anyway? No reason to think that it matters why love is not the same for everyone. It doesn't matter who prays for who. Love matters. Faith in love matters.

Zorel told me "Jesus loves you" when you were in your last days. I know he did. I know he does. The energy of love can never be denied. You showed me that when you closed your eyes so I could live. Your love showed me the faith I never knew existed. Your presence in my heart gave me the strength to lift my head without anger, guilt, and doubt that better days are coming.

Yes, Jesus loves me, my daughter and many other people said. They always wanted me to know that his love never dies. I didn't believe in this love, especially with you, Rocky, no longer by my side. Yes, she also said my Rocky loves me too; our Rocky loves both of us. She said your love is always alive. Now I know what she was talking about. Now I wrap my heart around that love and believe that everything is possible.

ROCKY

For so long, I have been trying to figure out how all those hopes and beliefs can grow inside such a little body. Why was my little girl was trying to soothe my pain? I am a grown-up. I should do that for her. But then I realized, she is your little sister. For a child like her, it doesn't take a village to raise her; it takes a dog's patience, protection, and love. With you, she moved as close to perfection as she could. She definitely couldn't achieve that with me or any other human being.

Today, as I watch her throwing a ball but refusing to run after it, I know she is happy because she feels your presence yet is sad for not being able to see you. She hopes, she prays for you to come back. When she connects to the universe, I know there is something so unique and powerful in her words; no adult can describe their wish as easily as a child like her can. No adult can believe so effortlessly but so profoundly. It's like lightning that strikes and goes away, strikes again, and goes away again. But this type of "lightning" is always peaceful and can't hurt anyone. This type of lightning doesn't go away. It's there to teach an important lesson: simple, grounded souls can reach high. Simple, grounded souls can give the future to this world. Simple, grounded souls can make miracles happen.

I hope and pray too, but I have more faith in her prayer than my own. I can still hear her telling me months ago, "Mom, don't let people stop Rocky's breathing; they don't know when the doors of Heaven are open. Only God knows that." Now that voice reminds me that the energy of love, the universe, our life's source, can do wonders even after the last breath and last goodbye. With belief, there is always a new beginning. Nobody deserves a new beginning with you more than her.

—Mom

Dear Zorel,

Let me tell you about your mom, as I knew her long before you were born. She would probably never admit this to you, but many things in this world take her peace away. She constantly worries whether she will be able to provide enough food, buy clothes and toys, cover school, entertainment, and unforeseen expenses. She worries that if something happens to her, nobody will pick you up from school; no emergency contact is on file. I don't blame her, as she wants you to have a better childhood and life than the one she had. Unlike me, who wags his tail every time you walk around, she often forgets that happiness is a two-way street; it takes two cheeks to smile and two hands to embrace. It takes the upper and lower lip to say "I love you." It takes your smile to reflect in her eyes and show her that everything will be okay.

Don't get me wrong. Parenting a child is not an effortless task. Especially when you have to do it all alone and when you have to play the role of every family member a child should but doesn't have. For someone who grew up with only a grandmother, with everyone else out of sight, she came a long way and still has a long way to go. She wants to give you the best life possible. She struggles but always reminds herself that she should never give up.

I know she often relies on me to bring a smile to your face. I do that for both of you. And gladly. I show her that when you stand in front of a person long enough and continue to make your face as cute as it can be, eventually, they will pay some attention to you. If you are lucky, they may even stroke your head. That doesn't mean they are going to like you, and perhaps they will turn away as soon as they notice that you are becoming too comfortable. Yet that doesn't mean everyone is like that. Some will stroke your head twice. Some will not bother to reach out at all.

If you keep walking away from people, you will have no one by your side when you need someone the most. You don't have to beg them for love; it is good enough when you get their attention without making them angry or sad. That means when you send out some positive energy, such energy always has the sender's return address on it.

Your mom loves me so much. I know that. I also know that I am the only living being she trusts entirely with you. Do you know that she kept repeating for hours and days, weeks, and months, "Why Rocky? Why did you take Rocky, God? We had only Rocky, God. Why Rocky?" I know she wants me back. She believes I'll come back and be with you again. What do you think, my dear Zorel? I already know, but I would like to hear from you. I want you to speak to me as you always did. In a loud voice. With a big smile. Extended hands. Legs ready to run. It's time for me to listen and for you to share your beliefs and wishes and also to boss me around.

Your Rocky

Dear Rocky,

I saw Mom crying so many times. Our house is empty without you. I often want to cry with her, but I don't. I don't want to let her know that her hiding spots are not hiding her well from a curious child like me. I usually wait for her to finish, dry her face, and put a smile on. Then I just come to her and say, "Mom, don't give up, Rocky's coming back."

I just wish to know when because I'm so impatient. Very, very impatient. I think and believe with my heart that you are coming back on my birthday. You know how much I love surprises; you will be my biggest.

You know, Rocky, I don't cry like I used to. I cry less, but I

still hurt a lot. My pain is the strongest when I see a dog that reminds me of you. I feel like crying every time I see a dog's head sticking out of a car window. I imagine you sitting next to me and doing the same thing.

These are the times I want to cry so badly, but Mom is watching me. I don't want to make her sad, so I look away. Still imagining you sitting next to me.

I miss going to the dog park with you and Mama. We were all happy there. We were family. Having you around was so good. Having you around again will be even better.

Miss you,
Zorel

April 26, 2021

Rocky, do you remember that day when you and I sat in my old Honda? It was late at night, and we had just left my friend's house and were on our way back home. Back to Grandma who waited for us. I started my car and immediately turned it off. I told you I had to get out and pray. I opened my door and stepped out. I went down on my knees with no shame of people around me and just prayed. I prayed while you watched. You were there, but my eyes were closed, and I couldn't see you. I didn't have to. I felt your presence in every word I said in my prayer. The same as I do now. But this time is different. This time we are praying together. We are praying for another walk together, another night swim, another run through the woods, another nap, and another embrace. And it's coming. It's coming soon. This is stronger than hope. This is faith. What's God's gift, nobody can take it away. I love you, Rocky.

—Mom

ROCKY

Dear Rocky,

Mom got so mad with me today. The lady from school called her and asked her if we were homeless. Mom said no. Mom asked why. The truth is I told all my friends and teachers that we had lost our home because I am sure that's true. Without you, we lost everything. Home. Family. Happiness. We can't even find a parking spot when we go somewhere. We are not as lucky as before. Nothing is the same. But I know lucky stars can and will come back. I know the school will not call Mammy again and ask her if we are homeless. And I'll not get in trouble. Mammy will be happy, not mad.

Zorel

May 2, 2021

It's past four in the morning. I'm sitting and looking out the window. It rained almost all day. Earlier I could hear thunderstorms off in the distance. I remember how afraid you were of them. So often, I wrapped my arms around you to help you feel safe. Still, you preferred to be next to Zorel. You felt safer with her. I know her hands and smile are warmer than mine, and I know her soul better matches your goodness.

Everything around me is swallowed by silence except my sobs. Today was one of those meaningless days for me. I know, I know, your beautiful eyes, like two lighthouses, are breaking through the dark. They would disagree that sadness can ever prevail. I know the substance of your being was always a joy. Tonight, I can't help but cry and move around like a wounded soldier. That's all I can do.

Every time I feel like this, I have doubts I'll ever see you again. I fear that's it. We had what we had, and I'll be hungry for your presence for the rest of my life. Maybe you didn't come to my dream for a long time because you want me to move on, just like me when you were taking your last breaths. You were lying down with your back facing me. I didn't stand before you because I was afraid I would beg you again to stay, not to leave me yet. I was worried you would try to go with my wishes despite all your pain. To obey a spoiled and selfish me, as you always did. I knew you were sedated when you took your last breath. Still, you could hear my voice, my crying. As people say, when the soul becomes one with the light, hearing is the last sense to leave the body.

Even on days like this one, I want to believe and have faith in your comeback. You didn't enter my dream because you are living in a different body, the one that's trying to find his old home. You are walking the Earth. Maybe somewhere nearby. You remember me. You can't forget me. God will shine the light on your path so you can return soon. On May 17, I imagine a miniature version of you standing at the door when I open it. You will be the best present for Zorel's birthday. You will be our proof that love never dies. It can't. Oh, how I miss kissing those sweet, soft ears. I miss everything about you, Rocky. I miss everything about you, my only genuine friend. I'm waiting for you. Waiting for you.

—Mom

May 4, 2:31 a.m.

Dear Rocky,

I think about every valuable lesson you taught me during our time together. Now, I finally know that you showed me what my life was, is, and what it can become. Your life was a reflection of my own, yet you handled everything differently, much better than me.

Let's start from the beginning. You were a tiny baby when I

approached your cage. The lady who worked there said, "Other dogs may growl or bark at him, but this pup just sits there and minds his own business. He's so mellow." You sat there, an unwanted little thing, and waited for someone to notice you. Just like me, three decades earlier.

When I picked you up and brought you home, I was ready to give you all the love I could. Just like my grandmother when she decided to raise me. But just like me, you ended up with someone who lived in misery. I responded to all those who betrayed me with a heart full of anger. My anger became my pain, which affected those I was living with—you and Zorel.

I became ill because of my thoughts and actions. My illness was taking me to the grave. But you switched places with me. You gave me life and more time with Zorel. How can I ever repay you for what you have done for me? I guess I can start by loving and respecting myself more. That's what you wanted me to do. That's what you taught me, Rocky.

—Mom

May 5, 2021

Today, once again, is one of those days. I can't focus on anything else but this big void left inside me. I have no doubt you will be back. A wise person once told me that if you want plan A to work, don't make a plan B. I don't. I plan to start another lifetime journey with you on May 17. I can hardly wait to be with you again. I miss those silky ears of yours. They were always my favorite thing to kiss. And I miss watching you roll in the grass, swim with that grin of yours, sitting next to me when I write, napping side by side with me. I love you. I love you so much.

—Mom

May 28, 2021

Dear Rocky,

Today was Zorel's last day of school. Can you believe she will be a second grader by the end of this summer? She is so grown now. A big and adorable girl. We missed you today so much because you were always there to share our accomplishments and happiness; when she was born, when I left an abusive relationship, when I got my master's in legal studies, and so on. With you, everything was better, more festive, and happier.

I know you took that joyride in the car with us. I was almost tempted to roll down the window for you. I chose not to because today was sweltering. Instead, I put the air conditioner on low so you and your sister could feel a nice breeze in the backseat. I cried when she said she missed you. I cried when she said she was still waiting for you even though her birthday had passed. It was a good thing I had sunglasses on. It was even better that my painful sobs are loud only in my mind.

Rocky, do you remember how we used to pick her up from school every day and then go to a dog park? Sometimes we just had a picnic in nature where you and she chased anything that moved. You preferred to chase ducks. She would go after deer and squirrels. Fun times.

As I promised you, I try to cry less and smile more. Thinking about happy times brings a smile to my face. All you left me with is beautiful. I'm thankful for that. I truly am. I always will be.

—Mom

June 1, 2021

Dear Rocky,

Since the day I set you free and allowed angels to help you fly high and far, I feel you are finally happy. I think you needed that kind of blessing from me. You waited for it for a very long time.

I must admit my selfishness is still present wherever I turn. I so much want to be in control that I ignore the damage associated with such behavior. I want and need you back, but I'm limited by my humanity. I have nobody to bargain with. Only myself. One side of me is content because you are free. The other is empty because you are not physically with me. Neither of them wants to negotiate with the other.

You are my life. You are my child. You saved me from others and from myself. I know you are still watching over me, but I feel so alone, unlovable, and worthless. I feel God gave me a chance for a happy life with you, but I screwed up. I let you suffer, and then I lost you. I couldn't save you. I was hurting you while prolonging your return to the stars where you belonged. I'm sorry, so very sorry for everything.

You are my faith. You are my hope. My inspiration for waking up every morning and finding a reason to smile every day. I continue living. I take every breath as peacefully as I can. I live in the moment like you taught me to. I want to be able to one day help a fellow human save their pet. I want to show them how to protect them before it is too late. I don't want them to lose a loved one in the way I lost you.

Rocky, I will be there with you no matter where you are. This time you have a leash I am attached to. I held your leash on Earth, but you were always leading me. I didn't mind. I enjoyed following you. I loved everything about you. I loved loving you. I never stopped.

—Mom

Dear Rocky,

I'm in your hometown now. Here in Dallas, everything reminds me of you. I know how much you loved the dog parks here, and I often feel guilty for moving you to Houston. Our beach adventures made me feel better when feelings of guilt became overwhelming.

I try not to talk about you with those I know. I talk to strangers instead. I show them pictures of you. They judge me less for missing you. I am a proud mom when they admire your beauty. You were indeed one of a kind.

Before our trip to Dallas today, I was on our patio getting something. I was in a hurry because you loved spending time out there; now it looks so ugly and empty. I can't stand being there. "Mom, Mommy," I heard repeatedly. I thought Zorel was calling me. When I turned and looked inside, I saw her packing her clothes. It wasn't her. "Mom, Mommy," I heard again. Nobody was around. Nobody but me and you. I knew you were there with me. You were getting ready to come with us to Dallas, which you loved so much, with the family that would never leave you behind, your soul family.

—Mom

Dear Rocky,

Let me tell you a little about our day. When I picked Zorel up from school, both of us were in a pretty good mood. She was so excited to share with me that one of her classmates wanted to trade his Pop-It (this is a new toy/fidget for kids that is supposed to keep them busy and calm) for her squishy toy. I like to see her smiling. Especially because she is sometimes too serious, and I worry. I know how much she misses you. But whatever I do to be patient and joyful like you were with her, I can't even come close to the relationship the two of you shared. But I try. You know. God knows too.

On our ride back home, I tried to sing to her. I don't know if my voice reminded her of your cute howls (my singing attempts often sound like that), but when I turned around expecting to see her smile, I found her crying. She told me she saw someone in the street with a dog that looked like you. She also told me she saw your star shining in the sky long ago. She hadn't had any dreams of you.

It has been ten months and fifteen days since she saw you for the last time, and she worries that she will never see you again. I wanted to comfort her and make her feel better, but my voice was breaking. My tears started falling. All I could do was hope that she didn't see them.

Again, you know we don't have anybody in this world but you. You also know that I talk to you every day. Sometimes silently. Sometimes aloud. I know you can hear me because I feel your presence, as I do now. Stay with Zorel. Stay with me. Always stay with us. We are a tiny, untraditional family, but rules and norms can't measure our love for each other. How can anyone measure something with no end?

When we arrived back home, a playful bark greeted us. The neighbor's dog's smile reminded me of your cheerful face. Zorel went down on her knees, extended her hand, and the puppy ran to her. She wiped her tears off and gently petted his fur. Heaven is not far. Heaven is never far. Not when you talk and listen to your angel. —Mom

---

A fight for the one you love never ends. It can't, as the only weapon you use is faith, and faith brings miracles every day, every hour, every breath. I was probably connected to Rocky long before he or I were born, yet I can only remember the life we shared for the past twelve-and-a-half years. We have learned so much from each other, but much more is left to learn. On my porch, I stand and wait for him because I believe that this time, he is choosing Zorel. When a dog has to leave a child, especially one growing up in an untraditional family, he goes with a plan to return. He knows where his heart is, as Jonny did decades ago, and no matter how beautiful Heaven can be, Earth is what he dreams about. Our new (earthly) journey is starting soon.

When you look at the sky, you will see many stars. There are about a septillion of them in the universe. If the light of one of them dies, nobody will notice. But if that's your star, you will know it. Your faith is your faith. You don't need to share it with the world, but you probably will because you want everyone else to know about your star. A star like yours never dies because faith can live both in darkness and light. What's the name of your star? As I said earlier, on May 17, 2008, I saw a puppy sitting in his cage. I learned his name was Rockstar, but everyone called him Rocky.

What's your soul telling you to do every day? What is your mission? People will have their opinions, and they should, but stay true to what's written inside your heart, not to what others think. Rocky taught me that brushing off negativity is beneficial for people and everyone around them. Throughout our nearly thirteen years together, he was attacked by other dogs on multiple occasions. Being a sixty-pound dog with wolf-like features and deep blue eyes, you would think no dog would ever stand a chance of winning a fight against him. Yet Rocky never attempted to fight back or defend himself. Sometimes he would just roll in the grass and ignore an angry animal. Of course, momma bear was always there to warn everyone not to mess with her boy.

Rocky's tail wagged when people tried to get into protective mode just because an "unfriendly beast" was passing by. Some kept their distance, while others changed their perceptions quickly. I was surprised he didn't pick up on the unfriendly attitude of people and tried to act accordingly, as I did. But now I know that once you have faith in love, it follows you everywhere. There is a difference between having faith in love and loving the feeling of having such faith. Other people often influence the latter because many like to tell you what your belief should be. They will even accept you into their "pack" if you comply. But anything that's not you, and only you, is unstable. It has so many conditions. It hurts. Dogs like Rocky are born with faith in love, and humans like me must learn it.

Life can be full of unanswered questions, but genuine faith doesn't and can't revolve around uncertainty. It is beyond anything, including life itself.

Rocky's breathing was heavy in the final hours of his life. I felt as if a mountain was pressing against my chest. I was waiting for the morning to make a call for in-home euthanasia. I was trying to hold his head in my palms, which seemed to help him close his eyes for a moment. But he didn't sleep. His body was shutting down. Around six a.m., he stood up and walked to the door. In the last hours of his life, my dog didn't forget that he was potty-trained. Once outside, I took him to an emergency room. In the hospital, I had a choice between selecting euthanasia and letting him pass on a cold table or sedating him and letting him pass at home. I chose the latter.

Rocky's last three breaths were so peaceful that I thought he was improving. When silence took over afterward, I thought he started breathing again. That was all hope. You can call it foolish hope. Desperate hope. A temporary escape from reality. I stayed close to him for hours. I kept asking myself how we could let go of someone we love dearly. I kept delaying allowing strangers to carry a huge piece of my soul away.

Hope is full of unanswered questions, and humans don't like to live with unanswered questions. I've been waiting for some closure for many months now. Something like having a dream of Rocky showing me beautiful heavenly colors. Like years ago, my grandmother showed me that a "better place" truly exists. But I wasn't lucky this time. No sign, no dream, nada, until I started unlocking doors inside of me and discovering faith; and faith, differently from hope, is all about certainty. My questions and prayers, one by one, were answered. That's when I knew that Rocky's coming back. His soul is. And since I'm a human and prefer to experience life with my five senses, he is coming to have another lifetime with me. His sister is ready to have her family all in the same place again.

Every day, I find a drawing of Rocky somewhere—in the living room, patio, or kitchen—but they are mainly on the floor beside my daughter's bed. Pictures of the two of them are everywhere. On the wall above Rocky's favorite cooling-down and chilling-out spot are the words *Enjoy Every Moment*. That's what Rocky never forgot to do—taking us on long walks so we had fewer opportunities to think of what we were missing in life and more opportunities to appreciate what we had. He was always up for some good times and adventure. With him, even the pandemic lockdown was full of wonder and silliness.

Although I know how much Rocky loved me, he avoided my presence when I was angry. One of the hardest things I had to admit while staring at the empty spot where he used to be (every single spot of my home was Rocky's spot) was that I spent years and years in an angry state of mind instead of an appreciative one. I spent many days and nights being angry or in the process of looking for some reason to be angry. Angry at myself for picking the wrong man to be the father of my child. Angry at a family member I love dearly for silencing their phone when the caller ID displays my name. Angry at my child for not finishing her food. Angry at a meteorologist for announcing that rain was expected.

Angry at angry people, whom I attracted like a moth to a flame as soon as I walked outside of my house.

The anger led to disappointment and sadness. I was down, down, and more down while Rocky used his soft fur, cold nose, and beautiful eyes to cheer me up. As any animal lover knows, dogs, of all living creatures, are the quickest at picking up on our emotions and energy. Of all living creatures, your dog knows you the best. My fur baby was definitely an expert at reading my mind and heart. He was always ready to take me outside to calm the storms that raged within my inner walls. He succeeded every time, even when I lost the person with whom I shared the most special bond—my grandmother.

Now I know I didn't deserve so much love and understanding. I didn't deserve a soul as pure as Rocky. I even blame myself for picking him up when he was a puppy and bringing him home. I often think that with a happier and calmer person, he would have had a better life. But each time I have similar thoughts, something inside me tells me that God had a reason for putting us on the same path. My heart knows that God now has a more substantial reason to give us another life together. That reason is Rocky's little sister.

Chapter Twenty-Eight
SIGN

Don't wait for the right people to come into your life; live today, live in this moment, and find a dog . . . he or she always waits for you somewhere.

September 26, 2021

 During one of my late-night meditations, I tried to stop my racing thoughts so I could open my heart and let love flow freely. Without any doubt, I knew that was the only way to have my soul connect to Rocky's. I longed for that, more than anything else. Soon, I felt his presence in the room. He was next to me. As always, he stretched out by my right side. I was at peace, reuniting with the love of my life, his spot no longer empty. But being just a human and desiring to see before I can believe, I asked for the evidence. I said, "Please, Rocky, give me some sign that this is truly you. Show me a stray puppy." After sending my request into another realm, I realized how silly my message sounded. I thought about it a bit and, a few moments later, tried to come up with something better, something more realistic. I took a deep breath and whispered, "Or you can show me one of those squeaky yellow balls you loved playing with. Send me one of them."

The next day, I took Zorel to a park we had never been to. As usual, she made friends immediately, and it was obvious that we would stay there for a while. It was Sunday, so we had nowhere to rush off to and nothing better to do. Two hours later, she was still a hundred percent into her play, and I was looking for something to do. I wanted to kill my time and let her enjoy hers, so I decided to go to the car and clean its interior. I found a plastic bag and started collecting trash: empty water bottles, broken toys, papers and some more papers, and soon the bag was full. While holding it, I glanced around, looking for a trashcan. At that very moment, our eyes met. In front of me stood a dog without a collar or leash. He looked like a Shar-Pei mix (Rocky was a husky and Shar-Pei mix).

I walked toward the dog, trying to locate her owner, but she ran away. Children, grownups—I asked everyone I came across if they knew whom the dog belonged to. Some told me they had seen her before, roaming around; others just shook their heads and walked away. One of the children pointed behind me. "I think there are two dogs," he said. "Two dogs?" I repeated, raising my eyebrows. I was surprised but wasted no time. I was on a mission to find the other pup and save them both.

It took me less than a minute to locate another dog; her little pal led me to her. They looked almost identical: medium-sized, light brown, with wrinkled skin around the face. They were both sitting in a big field, peacefully but with great curiosity, waiting for me to approach them. They let me pet and play with them. But I fell short every time I attempted to leash them and get them into my car. Soon, a police officer came to my aid. Nothing the two of us tried worked. The dogs were more interested in the "catch me if you can" game than anything else. For a few minutes, I just stood there, pondering what I should do and whom I should call to help me help them. That prompted me to dial an animal control phone number. To my disappointment, no one came, and I alone couldn't do much for them. It was already dark, and everyone except Zorel, me, another adult, and a child had left the park. I decided to return in the morning and put in another rescue effort for them. I felt neither of them had Rocky's soul, but they were undoubtedly the sign I asked for from him. A sign that he is always around. A sign that I must never think otherwise.

September 27, 2021

I picked Zorel up from school and drove to the park where we left the dogs. I was hoping animal control had picked them up. But I wasn't ready to leave them to the fate of an animal shelter. I didn't want them to get euthanized, like many other dogs, just for the space. I told myself I would search every pound and offer to foster the bonded duo if I found them. As if reading my thoughts, Zorel looked at me and said, "Mom, we have to take care of Allie One and Allie Two." Since yesterday, two dogs with wrinkled faces were no longer just some strays but two souls who had reserved spots in my child's heart.

We spotted them near the high school about two miles from the park. They were following a couple of students. I made a U-turn and parked in the school's parking lot. Zorel ran up to them and hugged them as if they were her long-lost puppies. "Allies, there you are." They wagged their tails, stopping for a moment, then continued walking. Unlike the previous day, exhaustion, hunger, and thirst were written on their faces. They were panting with their heads close to the ground and eyes desperately looking around and begging for help. I tried the school door, but it was closed, so I asked one student if she could go inside and get some water for them. In the meantime, Zorel and I returned to the car to get some canned food.

Half an hour later, the dogs had water and food and rested on the sidewalk. I took that time to speak with some school officials and asked them to contact animal control. I also made another attempt to reach them myself. An hour later, nobody came, and soon we would have to leave them. I was hurting deep inside because, once again, I couldn't find help.

Zorel didn't move away from the dogs. She kept trying to clean the mud around their bellies and feet. "Mom! What if one of them is Rocky? I miss him. I want to bring him back home." Her words stabbed my heart, but I didn't have to hide my tears because there were no tears in me. I didn't feel like crying because I was confident Rocky was with us and doing everything to keep Zorel and me strong. Through the interactions with those pups, he kept giving me signs he was there, watching over us. Two days ago, I asked for the proof, and he continued providing it. There was no doubt left in me that whenever this world tried to take my hopes away, my guardians from the spirit world would give me something to hope for. I would be okay. I would be fine.

September 28, 2021

I dropped Zorel off at her art class and drove to the high school where I last saw the dogs. I was glad that today I would be there alone. I didn't want to see my daughter sad again. I assumed the dogs were no longer there, and I knew she would be heartbroken. It was around four p.m., and the school's grounds were crowded. I drove around hoping to see two light brown, wrinkled heads with tiny flappy ears but found no trace of them. I took one more look before driving to the park where I saw them the first time.

When I arrived, I parked my car by the playground and began walking around the park. It was a Texas-style hot day, and soon I became thirsty and tired. Still, I continued, determined to check every place where they could hide from the heat. For the most part, the area was empty except for a couple of construction workers and a man jogging. I kept looking around, hoping to see them. I wanted to take down the disappointment that grew in me.

Finally, I slowed down and decided to ask my angel for help. "Where are they? What happened to them? Help me, Rocky. Please help them, Rocky." As I walked back to my car, I feared something terrible had happened to the pups, and a sudden wave of sadness and guilt hit me. I began walking faster, wanting to leave my surroundings as soon as possible, but before I reached my car, I caught sight of them coming out of a small bush. "There they are." I smiled, thinking of Rocky and how he had communicated with me lately. My plea was answered again.

I unlocked my car and took out a shopping bag full of dog food, treats, bowls, and bottled water. Moments later, when I approached them, they greeted me with puppy smiles on their faces, their tiny tails wagging from side to side. Their wet noses touched my hands, ready to inspect the goodies I carried.

Animal control never showed up, and after the third phone call, I figured it was pointless to reach out to them ever again. Once again, I couldn't get the dogs into my car, even with food and treats. I had to leave them behind. Another night for them on the street. Another night for me to pray for their safety. When I kneeled, one of them rolled over with all fours in the air, waiting for me to pet her. I thought about how much Rocky liked belly rubs while I felt her soft fur under my fingers. It felt like yesterday, and at the same time like decades had already passed since my boy was next to me like this. She closed her eyes, showing me how much she enjoyed my attention. I didn't want to leave them. I worried about them because it was going to rain that night and for the rest of the week. Where were they going to hide? What were they going to eat?

Rocky was afraid of rain and thunderstorms. He used to jump into Zorel's bed, put his head next to hers, and plead for her to comfort him until everything passed. My boy was communicating with me through these dogs, and I wanted to hear more. I never wanted this conversation to stop. I wasn't ready for this to end.

September 29, 2021

Today Zorel and I went back to the park, but the dogs were nowhere to be found. We first walked and then drove around, but they weren't there. The water bowl was still where I had left it a day prior. People were talking and children were playing, but I sensed some heavy silence in the air. *Oh my, am I getting attached to them?* I felt little pieces of guilt growing bigger inside of me. As usual, I started wondering what had happened to them. I imagined how different their lives would be if they were under our roof. Our home wasn't fancy, but they would be safe and loved until someone adopted them and offered them a permanent home. I kept thinking I could and should do more for them. They were vulnerable living beings. They needed someone to take care of them. And after all, they were the first "major" sign from Rocky.

Earlier that day, I had turned to social media to find a reputable rescue for them. But like many times before, people commenting were more interested in arguing with me than helping them. *Go help them. Who do you think you are to criticize animal control services in our city? Go feed them. Go trap them. Why didn't you provide the exact address so people can find them?*

I tried not to take hurtful comments personally. Some people are just ignorant or lack knowledge that animals, dogs in particular, can end up in the wrong hands. Not everyone sees them as precious souls who deserve nothing but love. *I hope we find them tomorrow. We will be back. Why do they have to be part Shar-Pei like Rocky? Why does one of them love belly rubs so much? We are coming again tomorrow. We are coming, babies.*

Again, the next day, Zorel and I will sit on the park's bench and hope the Allie sisters will show up from somewhere. We will come every day until they are safe. Rocky wants that. Zorel and I hope for that.

September 30, 2021

Nothing. Again, the dogs were not in the park. We drove and walked around, but we didn't see them. Even the water bowl wasn't there anymore. They seemed to be gone for good this time, and my worries multiplied. *Maybe they were hit by a car? Killed by some wild animal? Picked up by a person with bad intentions?*

The relentless heat could be fatal for them. For anyone. At one point, I thought I saw one of them lifelessly lying in the bushes (luckily, it was just a log), so I took my daughter's hand and led her in the opposite direction. Even the thought of her again witnessing the end of a life made it difficult for me to breathe. It was apparent they were no longer there, but we kept looking everywhere in the area. We were determined to find them.

We waited for about an hour in case they showed up, then drove to a nearby dog park. The dog park was empty. No cars, no people, no dogs.

"Let's go to that school again," Zorel said, still glancing around.

"Let's go," I said to her, trying to smile.

The high school's grounds were not as quiet as the park, but we didn't find the Allie sisters there either. "Baby, I think we should go back home," I said, touching Zorel's shoulder. She just nodded, lowering her eyes.

I took a different, alternative route to make the ride back home more exciting and to take both my and Zorel's thoughts away from the dogs. Less than five minutes later, I regretted that. While passing a long field next to the road, I noticed another stray dog. It limped and looked very thin.

I made the U-turn and parked my car on the nearby street. I quickly grabbed one of Rocky's leashes that I always keep on the passenger seat, and we hurried, hoping he was still there. We never found him.

Zorel started crying. Soon her sobs were getting caught in her throat. "He looked a lot like Rocky," she said as we walked back to our car. I moved closer to her, took her hand in mine, and we just stood there—two humans, feeling alone and unwanted in the world, like those dogs, lost souls.

I had no doubt in my mind that we had entered another "dog dumping area." "Maybe he got loose, and someone is looking for him." I tried to sound cheerful when we were back in the car. "We will come back tomorrow and search more for him and the Allie sisters." Zorel glanced at me, wiping tears off her face with her right palm. *One more time*; my thought was very loud. Then others, much louder, joined it. *I can't keep coming here. I can't keep bringing my child to this place. I want to keep my sanity. I can't do this anymore. I can't watch these innocent dogs wandering around, confused, scared, and hungry. I keep thinking I can save all of them. Not true. Not at all. But I may save one. I'll let Rocky decide that tomorrow. I know he will choose what's best for us.*

October 1, 2021

I kept my promise. We were at the park again, dog food in the bags and Rocky's leash on the passenger seat. Zorel was excited. Some of the first words she said to me when I picked her up from school that afternoon were, "We are going to look for dogs."

This time, the park was crowded, but the dogs we were looking for were not there. "Somebody picked them up," Zorel said after we spent hours walking and looking for them and then sitting and just waiting. I nodded, my eyes fixed on a little creek nearby. I avoided meeting her eyes because I didn't want her to see how much I looked forward to seeing our two friendly buddies again. "Let's go

to that school again," I said, trying to shake off her disappointment. "I think we will find them there."

After driving around the school for some time, I had to wrap up this pup hunt and return home. However, this is not where the story ends, as we saw two other dogs on our way back home. I was able to leash one of them, but he managed to get away; another one was gone even before I could come closer.

You see, sometimes you move to a beautiful city, hoping for a fresh start and a new home, but then you realize you will never be happy in a place where dogs are treated like non-living objects. You also realize that any city—any community that allows hungry, sick, and scared dogs to live on the streets—wouldn't treat people much better. You can often find people and dogs roaming the streets together. You can often see them being pushed away. If that is hard for you to bear, as it is for me, you'll know that your heart still hasn't found what it is looking for. It would be best to keep moving. Keep looking. That's why I keep moving. That's why I'll never stop looking.

Rocky wanted me to move to San Antonio, and I knew I would soon find out why. Even after being unable to save any of the dogs I came across, I am grateful he showed me the sign—not just one but one after another. This gave me some peace. I felt much more hopeful about his return. And I felt and still feel much more confident that I know when his spirit walks beside me and I can talk to him about everything. He listens, he cares, and above all, he knows there is so much more in life we need and will share. My heart feels that. Zorel's heart feels that. After all, the power of love is connected to the power of belief. They are beyond all senses and any explanation. They are everything, and everything through them is possible.

But the physical world never forgets to wound our wings if we try to fly too far from it. It was one of those days when I didn't even want to reach for help in a higher realm. Nothing worked or seemed right without seeing Rocky next to me. I cried before picking up Zorel from school. Zorel cried in the car. Pain is so contagious, and each of its grips is so tight, preventing a person from catching a full breath. Everything has been cut in half since Rocky doesn't take us to places full of nature and empty of people. We don't want to go to shopping malls, crowded events, or parties; we want to go where he took us, where he liked to go.

When I asked Rocky to send me a stray puppy as a heavenly sign from him, my little four S's—stubborn, sweet, silly, and smart furry child, as I loved to call him—he sent me two of them. And every time I thought I was seeing the Allie sisters for the last time, I kept finding them, and they kept bringing back more memories of my boy. One of them acted very much like Rocky. I enjoyed watching her while she was trying to play with a duck. She didn't give up, even though the bird wanted nothing to do with her. She stretched her front paws on the ground, held her behind in the air, and waited.

Then she jumped toward the bird, again and again. But when the duck turned toward her and started chasing her, she wasted no time escaping the angry bird. I watched her peeking at me from behind a tree, and I didn't know if I should smile or sit down and cry. It felt like I was watching old memories of Rocky and building new ones. I never knew seeing someone leaving the Earth and then witnessing their presence everywhere afterward was possible.

When the duck was far enough away, the dog returned and sat in the grass, holding her head high. She was proud of "defeating" the warrior. She was also proud because even from a distance, she could feel how much I admired her sweet face—especially that long and chubby Shar-Pei nose that was similar to Rocky's. Even though he was more on the husky side, his nose revealed the other breed. I liked to joke and tell people that my daughter Zorel inherited my dark eyes and my son Rocky got his long, "fat-boy" nose from me. His, of course, was much cuter than mine.

The dog was still soaring high with pride. I smiled, petted her sister, and then walked toward her. When I approached her, I squatted beside her and gently placed my hand on her fur. She immediately laid down on her back and offered me her soft belly. I obeyed gladly and started rubbing it up and down. She just closed her eyes and relaxed. I enjoyed being close to her, but it also felt weird being in the presence of a dog who wasn't Rocky. I realized that I almost forgot I could give someone such joy and peace and receive them in return. But that didn't last long, as I had to leave to pick Zorel up from her art class. I didn't know if they would be there tomorrow, but I knew I would keep coming and looking for them.

This experience reminded me of a picture that reads: *Enjoy Every Moment*. With Rocky still there, I didn't know that every moment is the first and last moment of something. I didn't know moments themselves make the entire life. The moment when we take our first breath. The moment when we feel that we are here to stay forever. The moment when we finally know that all we have is just a moment. Just one moment.

Even though I didn't feel that either of the Allie sisters had Rocky's soul in their beautiful, youthful bodies, I felt so guilty and sad for not being able to save them from a harsh street life. But there were other dogs, other signs from Rocky. Like that beautiful, blue-eyed shelter dog named Trua that I wanted to foster; she was euthanized before I could make a phone call. Or the dog I saw on one side of the road, but as soon as I pulled over, was no longer anywhere in sight.

Those dogs come and go, just as everything in life comes and goes. My thoughts, feelings, and wishes. Everything changes so quickly, except that I miss Rocky every second. Zorel is the same. She often looks up to me for comfort while I am trying to collect broken pieces of myself. I was abandoned as a baby. I experienced many types of neglect and abuse later in life. Then I grew up and attracted people who neglected and abused me even more. I lost my unborn child. I lost my grandmother, the only caregiver I ever had. I lost my home. I lost my country. I lost many furry friends who meant so much to me. All of that was painful and heavy, but watching Rocky take his last breath and close his eyes felt like my own death. No, it felt worse.

October 8, 2021

Zorel and I were in the area of the park where we saw the dogs two weeks earlier, and I felt a powerful urge to go back and look for them again. At the same time, I was afraid. Afraid to see the disappointment in my daughter's eyes if the spot where we left them was still empty. Afraid to think of what had happened to them. Again, so many maybes raced together with my thoughts. *Maybe they were picked up by animal control and euthanized, as is common for stray dogs with no family to reclaim them and no one to adopt them. Maybe someone caught them and used them as dog bait. Maybe someone poisoned them. Maybe they starved to death. Maybe they didn't survive the merciless heat.*

Half an hour later, Zorel and I arrived at the park and started looking around. We hoped to see the two cuties walking toward us, wagging their little tails. "Allies!" Zorel called out. "Allies, come." Soon she stopped, glancing at me and pointing not too far from us. "I think I see them; they're right there in the shade."

I glanced toward a pavilion where a group of people were having a party. I could see two dogs lying on the ground, but I assumed they belonged to them. "They're probably their dogs," I said to Zorel. "Let's go check." My daughter insisted on taking my hand and leading me to the dogs. I didn't mind. I was actually getting excited about potentially seeing them again.

Sure enough, as we were getting closer to the pavilion, I smiled and Zorel ran to pet our "lost and found" friends. "We found them. We found them," she said, jumping up and down as if she had won the most beautiful prize in the world. I hadn't seen her so happy in a very long time. Looking at the dogs, I hadn't seen a stray dog so excited to see us as they were.

I walked back to the car and took out a bag of dog treats I kept there since our first encounter with the dogs. Zorel followed me and grabbed the two red bags from me before I could close the car door. "I'll give them," she said, running back to them.

A few minutes later, we discovered that the Allie sisters were not alone. A gorgeous German shepherd-looking dog peeked at us from behind some nearby bushes. Right away, I noticed how much he resembled Rocky. I tried to get closer to him, but unlike the two sisters, he was very timid and preferred to keep his distance. He moved away and sat under a big tree. I approached him slowly, and while talking to him in a soft voice, I took my phone out of my pocket to take a picture of him. He glanced at me and turned his head to the side as if trying to show me that he was aware of his cuteness and would let me take a few shots of him. I grabbed that opportunity as quickly as I could. *You beautiful creatures; you deserve so much more and so much better in life,* I thought.

When I moved closer and kneeled right before him, still talking in a gentle voice, I expected him to stand up and leave. He had had enough of me, I assumed. To my surprise, he stayed in the same spot. Looking at him from a close distance, I realized he was the same dog Zorel and I saw walking on the side of the road. A limping puppy. The same dog I wanted to pick up, but who ran away. Now he allowed me to admire his beauty as long as I didn't try to reach for him. I was grateful for the time he chose to spend with me.

Chapter Twenty-Nine
COMFORT

As long as you live, your shadow will follow you. Your dog will be your shadow as long as he lives and beyond.

I procrastinate. Have all my life. I was working on one of Rocky's books for years. He usually slept beside my feet, occasionally lifting his head to remind me I should take a break. Sometimes, I could glance at him and scratch him behind the ears. I loved that. I also loved that he always showed me when he didn't want to be petted anymore by standing up and finding a spot where I couldn't reach him. Healthy boundaries are about respect and understanding, and no one could demonstrate them better than Rocky. That was Rocky's way of saying I needed to go back to work, and he needed to go back to sleep (in his golden years, Rocky preferred to sleep *in privacy*).

He knew I was writing a book about him; I could feel that. I could see in his eyes that he was content when I was content and how much he loved being my muse. I believe dogs know much more than we people do. They rely on the truth that frees, while we rely on the ego that imprisons.

Rocky was proud of me and consistently tried to show that I shouldn't write on and off but write every day. Writing is my greatest passion, after all. He knew that. With the poetry and "dog quotes" book, I took frequent breaks and started researching dog photographers who could best capture the beauty of my furry model. On September 18, 2020, everything changed. After Rocky's cancer diagnosis, I forgot about the book, and the photographer I hired was no longer for silly pictures of my boy but for his last pictures. Here is part of that (unfinished and unedited) book as a reminder that we should live as tomorrow might never come.

- Canine sense of smell is 1,000,000 times better than that of humans, but regardless of your breath in the morning, your dog's nose is the first thing that lands on your chin.
- People have tongues to talk; dogs have tongues to do everything else.
- People are exploring with the intention to own; dogs are exploring with amusement and love.
- Dogs will heal you and be there by your side to listen and care, especially if they know you are allergic to cat hair.
- The universe is happy every time the young mind that nobody understands meets a furry ear that listens with no judgment.
- Dogs and books can bring a lot of peaceful moments.
- People are praised for one act of kindness, but a dog spends his lifetime beside the most complex creature on the Earth—a human—loving them, and very often such kindness goes unnoticed.
- Dogs don't need to go to school to learn to do something; dogs' knowledge is based on emotions that people are often discouraged from bringing to work.

- A dog is a family you choose.
- A dog will never remind you that you were late, because he is ready to spend all his life waiting for you . . . to come back home; to feed him; to take him for a walk; to share a gentle touch and word with him; to receive all that attention and love he stores for you.
- A dog is the best companion when you feel sad, happy, alone, crazy, or simply tired of doing nothing—awesomely lazy.
- A dog is the best leader; he will let you hold a leash, but he will always be in control.
- Having someone to cover your back is good when you are not having good luck.
- A paw can very quickly put together pieces of a broken heart.
- Listen with your eyes and react with your heart; a dog can teach you a lot.
- A dog helps you get back on your feet. But not only that, a dog makes you believe you can fly.
- Dogs are simple, love is simple; loving dogs is simple because they are simply lovable.
- Dogs are the best. End of story.
- Be nice to your dog. He has seen all your "bad hair" days. Many people would not survive such a traumatic experience. (picture to be added: Rocky's surprised look)
- People live for paper—money, diplomas, marriage certificates, tickets here, tickets there. The only connection a dog has with paper is a tree. (picture to be added: Rocky marking his territory—a big tree)
- A human's world is made of material things. For dogs, people are the only connection to the material world. (picture to be added: Rocky's surprised look while I am

standing in front of him wearing my giant bunny slippers)
- Hard work pays off; a dog makes any work more manageable than it appears. (picture to be added: Rocky with piles of paper around him)
- Dogs are angels living on Earth; people are angels living in Heaven. (picture to be added: Zorel and Rocky giving each other a high five)
- People will listen to you while thinking about what they are going to say in response; a dog will listen to you while waiting for what you will say next. (picture to be added: Rocky's listening expression)
- People follow the rules, procedures, signs, and so on. A dog only follows his heart. (picture to be added: Rocky with a flower in his mouth)
- The healthiest meals have the simplest ingredients. The best ingredients for a healthy relationship are petting hands and a wagging tail. (picture to be added: Rocky enjoying belly rubs)
- Dogs listen and follow. They lead and care; no matter what, to love without conditions, they dare. (picture to be added: Rocky sleeping between Zorel and me)
- How can an entire world fit in one dog's heart, but the entire world can't love one dog? (picture to be added: Rocky's head sticking out a car's window; the smiling expression on his face shared with everyone)
- Choose your best friend wisely. (picture to be added: Rocky in his "sit for treat" pose)
- A dog's eyes are the coziest home on Earth. (picture to be added: focal point—Rocky's two-colored eyes)
- The best way to connect with nature and find inner peace is to take a dog for a walk. (picture to be added: Rocky, Zorel, and I walking in nature)

- No matter his age, a dog is always a little child—whatever you do and whatever he does, he needs to be next to you. (picture to be added: Zorel reading a book and Rocky sitting next to her)
- Dogs sponge off our thoughts and feelings. Don't make them worry; don't drag them into humanity. Instead, let them show you the beauty of simplicity, positivity, and pure joy. (picture to be added: Rocky swimming toward a ball)
- How come we have a list of things in the morning to do to get ready for the day, and a dog just stretches, stands up, and is ready to go back to sleep? (picture to be added: Rocky yawning and stretching)

The Simplicity of Being a Dog

A dog does not have a closet full of jumpers, shirts, and pants he will never wear. In winter, spring, summer, and fall, his fur he will have.

A dog takes the same shoes when he runs, goes for a walk, or a pet store.
NONE!!!
A dog does not have thousands of thoughts per day.
One will do,
And that one is . . .
YOU!!!

Dogs, Dogs, Dogs

When they come across bark, bark, bark
Some dogs become spark, spark, spark.

When they hear some loud tap, tap, tap,
Some dogs jump in your lap, lap, lap.

And when children dance, dance, dance,
All dogs wait for their chance, chance, chance.

Chapter Thirty
PAST LIFE REGRESSION

I'm perfect. I'm the light of the universe. I'm the center of my dog's world.

While working on the last pages of this book, I felt the urge to find a hypnotherapist and book a session for a past life regression. Deep in my heart, I felt this was one last thing I had to do before completing Rocky's book. During my session, I sat in a chair with my eyes closed, aiming for intense concentration. Images of what I was told were my previous life started appearing before me. But what I saw, in some ways, resembled the life I am living right now: my daughter is called *Mama,* and I am surrounded by animals rather than people. She looks happy. I seem to worry about something.

My name is Mary. I am a tall African woman wearing simple but beautiful colorful clothing. My job is to bring water to a nearby village devastated by fire. I carry big buckets every day. Helping those people is my passion and my purpose in life. They depend on me, but other than that, there is no emotional attachment between us. No friendship. They think I am a weirdo who doesn't belong in their world.

I became pregnant because I was violated (by someone who is my family member in this life), but I love my child dearly. I love our life in the forest. I am content. I love the sense of freedom I have there. I love the beauty of nature. Two significant animals in my life are a cow that stayed near me when I was a tiny baby and a monkey that followed me everywhere when I grew up.

The hypnotherapist's soothing voice signified the close of my session. "Now we are going to the moments when your soul began leaving your body. Can you tell me where you are? What are you feeling?"

"Beach. I'm lying on the beach. Sea corals surround me."

"Do you know you are dying?"

"Yes."

"Is anyone with you?"

"No . . . Sea corals."

"What about them?"

"Every time I see one, I feel ill. This time, there are so many around me."

When my session was over, I kept thinking about sea corals. I saw them in my dreams every time I was suffering. This started in my childhood. The last time I dreamed about them was on September 18, 2020. That was when Rocky was diagnosed with cancer.

I tried to find out what the animals I saw during my session represented, and I was astonished by my findings. A cow represents motherhood, caring, and life itself. On the other hand, a monkey represents joy, knowledge, and wisdom.

I attended my past life session with certain expectations. I wanted to know if Rocky was with me in my previous life, and I felt his soul in both animals, especially the monkey. My session confirmed the simple but most important thing—Rocky's love. His generosity, joy, and knowledge have followed me from one life to another. Regardless of time and space, Rocky is always with me.

Regardless of time and space, Rocky is teaching me about forgiveness. In my previous life, I forgave those who wronged me by loving my child. I am working on forgiveness in this life by learning to love myself.

Chapter Thirty-One
GIFT

A dog doesn't have to give you a gift, ever; a dog is a gift itself, forever.

What does God, the universe, or the heavens (or whatever you want to call something that we can only understand and embrace with a nonjudgmental heart) do for those who lose their only family? It restores their faith in miracles. That's exactly what happened with Rocky, Zorel, and me.

On October 13, 2021, we went to our usual spot to feed stray dogs. But instead of the two Allie sisters, we found three pups. The beautiful German shepherd was back with them. The food we brought wasn't enough for this ever-growing pack. "Time to go shopping for some more canned food and treats," I told Zorel as she played and ran with the dogs. She reluctantly agreed, and we drove to a nearby store.

Twenty minutes later, we walked toward our car with two bags of goodies. As I was about to put the food in my trunk, I noticed a dog walking toward a woman whose car was parked next to mine. He had no collar and seemed to sniff around for anything he could eat. "Is this your dog?" I asked her. She shook her head. "No, he's not." Then she turned to the dog standing next to her and murmured, "I've got nothing." She walked to the store without saying anything else.

I grabbed my shopping bags from the car and called the pup, who came to me with his tail wagging. I filled a paper plate with food and watched him gobble it so quickly it was gone in seconds. But when Zorel started talking to him, he seemed to forget about everything else; in a split second, he was on his back, waiting for her to start petting him. As I filled the plate again, the rain started pouring. In that very instant, the four-legged pal figured out it was not such a bad idea to jump into our car. The three of us—Zorel, the dog, and I—took off. And our ride began.

"This is Rocky. Rocky came back to us, Mom. Look at him." I could read happiness in my daughter's eyes; her smile brought a smile to my face. I was happy for her but still struggled to find joy in my heart. Perhaps children are never afraid to believe and love right away. With us adults, that doesn't come easy. And if you were hurt many times in your life, maybe never. Children know that dreams can become a reality one day, so they are always ready to embrace and cherish a new opportunity. Children and dogs need no words to understand what's happening around them.

Sure enough, our visitor followed Zorel wherever she went. He started playing with her like Rocky used to do. "Chase me, chase me, and then we're switching roles." He barked for her attention like Rocky used to do. He rolled on his back like Rocky used to do. My heart still didn't know what to think about all of that. My mind kept reminding me that the skeptic in me should never stop questioning.

After taking him on his first walk, we couldn't get him to the second floor because he refused to come near the stairs. His entire body would freeze each time I tried to move forward. It was already late, and my neighbors were not around to help me carry him, as they had done earlier that day. I had to do it alone. This took me back to 337 days and 8 hours ago when I carried Rocky for the last time when we came back home from the emergency room. Rocky was sedated. I struggled to bring him to the second floor. I needed someone's help. Zorel went knocking on our neighbors' doors. First door. Nothing. Second door. Nothing. And another and another. Until someone came out. I sat on the ground, holding Rocky. I could feel his heart beating hard, and I whispered into his ears, "It's okay. Everything will be okay." His fear subsided because he trusted me. He had faith in my love. "Help us, please help my dog," I cried to a man standing on his porch. Without saying a word, he did.

Rocky had faith in my love from the beginning. When, as a tiny puppy, he looked down the stairs, unsure of what to do, he stood next to me and waited. I took a step, and he followed. I took another one. He did the same. Then we ran. I smiled. He was wagging his tail. Loving him was always so easy. It still is.

Now, I am lifting this dog. He is in my arms, and his entire body is shaking. He even whines. He trembles. I am whispering to him, "It's okay. Everything will be okay." Our eyes meet for the first time, and I feel that I have seen that loving look before. It doesn't surprise me that he calms down right away. I know he knows that he is in good hands—better and stronger hands than those that held him before. Ginger, as my daughter calls him, trusts me. Like Rocky and Jonny, he looks a lot like a German shepherd.

I am looking at his face; the fur around it is grayish, just like Rocky's in his golden years. But he is still a puppy. His long nose and deep, loving eyes are almost touching my face. I feel his breath and heartbeat. My entire inner world celebrates his life. I carry him, and the universe holds both of us. It feels good to have hands full of love.

Our family is complete now. "I'm happy, happy, happy," Zorel sings as she runs with him around our apartment. "Rocky is back. He loves me, loves me, loves me." Then she runs even faster. "Hey,

ROCKY

Ginger, don't eat my shoe. Hey, Ginger, I love you, love you, love you, too."

One of the most important lessons I've learned from Rocky is that a child and a dog can have such a strong bond that nobody and nothing can break it. Yes, they will be separated someday (physically) from one another, but again, physically, they will be together. Jonny had been with me since my birth, but he had to leave me only days later. Three decades later, Rocky came. Rocky welcomed my daughter into this world. At the age of six, she watched him take his final breath. Less than a year later, Ginger found his way to my child's open heart and arms. Once again, we are a little untraditional family, but there is nothing I am more grateful for and proud of than us walking through life together.

We are picking up where we left off. The neighbor in Houston helped me carry Rocky inside my home for the last time. The neighbor in San Antonio helped me bring Ginger inside my home for the first time. Rocky spent his final hours watching Zorel's every step. Ginger spends his first hours in his new home following Zorel wherever she goes. I feel like I will have to wake up from my dream and face the truth. Happy endings exist only in fairy tales, only in fiction, not real life. I keep trying to convince myself. The only thing that tells me otherwise is this book. Somewhere between these pages, months and months ago, I mentioned one important reason that would bring Rocky back. Ginger is glued to that reason. The reason is Zorel.

In the past eleven months, I realized Rocky has been waiting for me to show him I am ready to trust in myself as he has always believed in me. When I achieve that, he will be back. He doesn't mind carrying the heavy load of this material world once again. He would do that for his family. Now it is my turn to show, to tell everyone willing to listen that regardless of the burden this world puts on our shoulders, we will never lose what we earn with love. And while I know I could never match Rocky's beautiful heart and unconditional love, I learned something essential from him: if you want to make the world a better place, become a better person; if you're going to help others find their way, find your own way first.

The last holiday we celebrated with Rocky was Halloween. Halloween is our first holiday with Ginger. Rocky was a "strict" police dog (more than once), Ginger is a "little" Red Riding Hood.

Sometimes I just want to ask a stranger on the street if they believe that even the most unique and unconditional love can repeat itself. I am not talking about similarities here—I am referring to continuity, which can be described as repetition. And I don't care what they will think about me; I simply don't care. Not anymore. Because I am confident that all I am experiencing right now is so true and so amazingly beautiful, and I want to share it with everyone else. But, like with everything else, you must believe it to receive it. A miracle happens every day, and everyone has a different name for it. My miracle is called Rocky.

Someone asked me how one can have confidence in themselves and share with the world something that doesn't fit in the "regular bucket." My answer is simple: If you are not confident sharing the truth, whatever you have to say will not fit in any "bucket." Soon after Rocky stopped breathing, I felt he started living again. *I was wrong,* I thought, *it can't be.* By doing so, I tried to stay in an acceptable belief zone. According to that belief, once life ceases inside our physical body, everything, including our own existence, is gone forever. In those moments, I was unaware that about 200 miles away from me, a new life started in a dog mother's womb. If you consider that dogs are pregnant somewhere between sixty and seventy days and that the vet told us on October 22 (a little over eleven months since Rocky's passing) that Ginger was between eight and ten months old, it all makes sense. Now I know that seeing Rocky breathing again on November 10, 2020 wasn't my grief-accumulated delusion but the reality that took place in a different city. At that time, I didn't know I would move from Houston to

San Antonio just to pick that puppy off the street. When our paths crossed, I was still deep in grief, looking for any sign from the spirit world, and he was a puppy looking for food. I fed him and was ready to walk away. He wasn't. He couldn't leave my daughter's side. Now they follow each other everywhere. And every night, I listen to his breathing and study his face while he sleeps. I know he is my boy. A mother can recognize her child, no matter where and no matter what. I recognize Rocky no matter where and no matter what.

As someone who is still in the early stage of animal communication learning, I continue practicing, trying to connect to Rocky and asking him about Ginger. Even though this handsome boy behaves like Rocky's twin brother, this never-completely-satisfied-human keeps asking for more signs, more proof. One day, while sitting in a deep meditative state, I asked, "Rocky, if your soul is in Ginger's body now, show me a green light. If not, show me a red light." The ringing of my phone interrupted me and prompted me to open my eyes. I looked at the unknown number and, for a couple of moments, considered answering the call, but I let my phone ring until it stopped.

When silence took over, I took a deep breath and positioned myself comfortably for the second time. But as I was about to close my eyes again, I remembered the question I asked just a minute ago ". . . green light . . . red light." Then it hit me. Rocky was trying to answer my question. *But I didn't press the green or red button*, I thought. *What now? Green light. Red light. Green light. Red light.* Then I heard my inner voice telling me "Go with what all your animal communication teachers instructed you." *Respect the first thought, the first feeling that came to your mind, and don't worry if it makes no sense right away. It will. Give it time. Be patient. Show gratitude.* I told myself "Even though you never answered the call, you initially wanted to do so. Your pup knew that. Your dog knows you better than anyone else. He is next to you right now. Don't worry about anything. Wipe your tears away and let yourself be happy again."

On our third day with Ginger, we visited a dog park, and what else would Zorel and her dog do there other than play fetch? Watching them together is joyful. "Mom, come here," Zorel yells toward a bench where I sit. "Hurry up," she pleads while smiling and reaching high. When I approach her, she points at the sky. A mesmerizing rainbow is spread before us.

It is there even if we don't see it. You are tall enough to reach it if you stand with your heart open to love. A child and a dog are reaching for it right now, and I am ready to join them, to join my pack. Nothing feels better than watching your dream come true. When you keep falling and ask the universe to carry you, it will. Embrace the strength of that closeness; embrace that connection with a smile, like Zorel and I are embracing Rocky.

One of the people Rocky sent my way when my grief was the strongest was a beautiful soul and a talented writer, Tina Proffitt. Her book *Come Back* helped me cope with unbearable pain. I contacted Tina soon after reading her book, and a few emails and one phone call later, I felt like I had found a new friend. So, after bringing Ginger home, I couldn't wait to share the news with her. I sat down and wrote her this email.

> Dear Tina,
>
> When we ask the universe to bring us family and friends, the universe will answer. Definitely. These words best describe my response to your last email. I can't adequately express how much I appreciate the picture of your beautiful fur babies you shared with me and your kind words. This made my day! For some

reason, I considered you my friend as soon as I read your book, and I am so glad to get in touch with you.

Going back to my first sentence, I have to share something with you. Last week I went to feed the stray dogs I told you about and instead of finding two of them, I saw a third one, which I soon figured out joined their pack. So I went to the store to buy more food and then another dog came to me. This one took food from me but seemed to be more interested in my daughter than anything else. On that particular day, it started raining, and looking at him like he was some lost, fearful, and hungry child, I opened my car's door and offered him shelter. He didn't seem to mind.

Long story short, he is still with us—checked for a microchip and fully vetted (just in case). The thing is, he's acting a lot like my boy that I told you about, especially when he's around my daughter. He also looks a lot like him. I often see my dearest boy in his eyes and I am afraid that my imagination is just taking over. What surprises me the most are people, strangers we come across, who indicate that I have the best babysitter in the world.

Lately, I've been trying (so hard) to connect with my pup and ask him if his soul has anything to do with this dog, but I am not getting any clear answers. There is a lot of confusion and excitement in me right now. Most of all, I am happy for my daughter. There is so much joy in her eyes when she is interacting with this dog and so much pride in her voice when she says, "I told you my brother would be back."

I've attached a picture of the dog. We were outside the other day and my daughter called me to show me the rainbow. I can't even describe how I felt at that moment. There were so many questions and so much gratitude in my heart. The rainbow of my fur child watching over us or my other angels watching us and being happy that we are back together? Who knows?

Dear Tina, I am sorry for such a long email. If you find time, please give me feedback on this. Any suggestion or advice would be greatly appreciated as I have nobody to talk to about this, nobody who will understand. I am sure this has something to do with my furry child, but I am not certain how or in what way. I will do anything to know . . . For the first time, I am even considering seeking help from an animal communicator and trying to find out . . .

I still feel all this is just a dream, or I just imagine things. Especially now when I am writing the last pages of my book. I keep asking myself if this experience is the ending I have been waiting and hoping for—Happy Ending!

Dear Anna, my new friend!

The first thing I wanted to say was that I wanted to take time to think about your email before I replied. I wanted to be able to give you a well thought-out answer.

Second, I truly believe that what your daughter already feels is the truth, that her brother has returned to her. And he is the best babysitter in the world, one who loves her!

Third, that beautiful rainbow in the sky above him seems to only solidify that he has returned at the moment when your book has reached its culmination! It is as if he is saying, you have been on the right track, what you are doing is so important!

Isn't it wonderful, the way you met him again? Destiny at work is a beautiful thing!

Fourth, my advice is to trust yourself. Trust your inner feelings. And know that I believe that he brought the rainbow to you to let you know that it is in fact him. Your intuition is very strong and worthy of your trust.

Last, I too have asked the universe to bring me friends, and one of the answers has been you, a fellow author, who loves dogs as much as I do. I'm so pleased that you felt a connection just from reading my book. I look forward to reading yours!

Please never hesitate to contact me with anything you want to talk about.

Be well. I look forward to hearing from you soon and getting a report on how your new family member is settling into his home again.

Your Friend,
Tina

I was never confident enough to say I could bear anything this life threw at me. I will tell you why. When Rocky was in the last moments of his life, I sat next to him, but I wasn't looking into his eyes. On our little sofa, we were sitting in this exact order: my daughter, myself, and Rocky with his back turned to us. I was making some not-so-important phone calls to distract myself from the reality that was pushing me deeper and deeper inside the dark wall. We were like a hammer and a tiny nail.

At one point, Rocky's labored breathing calmed down, and I foolishly started believing that all the steroids and pain relief injections he had received in the emergency room were making him feel better. Not long after that, he lifted his head as if searching for me. I was unsure if he opened his eyes because they were closed minutes ago. I didn't stand up. I didn't hug him and tell him "everything will be okay, I love you" as I should have. I could only put my hand near his belly as he always liked me to do and pet it. I couldn't face him or the truth. Deep inside, I knew that was it; the end had come. In those moments, I could find many explanations for that. I didn't want him to stay any longer in his body and prolong the pain and suffering. I wasn't ready to see fear and pain in his eyes. I didn't want to scream and loudly weep and beg him to stay, beg God to let him stay. What I was unwilling to admit was that I feared my heart wouldn't be able to take that, and besides losing her furry brother, Zorel would lose her mother. At six years old, she would lose her entire family, and neither Rocky nor I wanted that fate for her.

What makes me different today, maybe stronger too, is that I know helping someone doesn't mean keeping them alive. I didn't choose euthanasia for Rocky. I learned this lesson the hard way by not preventing all that agony he went through. One of the reasons I became a Reiki practitioner is because I believe proper energy flow can ease one's passing and one's grief.

Rocky was always a peacemaker in our home. That's why he brought Reiki into my life. He showed me he is at peace now through many the dreams and messages he sent me. He wanted me to find my peace and help others discover theirs. He tried to take me off the long path full of anger and worries, show me how to trust in love, and go with the flow.

Lying on a massage table with my eyes closed, having my second Reiki session, brought tears to my eyes. One thought kept circling in my mind: *Rocky wants me to live. Rocky wants me to live.* Grief took a heavy toll on my emotions, body, and soul. I felt like I had to learn to live without legs and arms, in tears, and without hope, faith, and love. Rocky wanted to save me by placing information about Reiki before me. Even the skeptic in me reached for it. I became interested. I wanted and needed to learn more. And when I did, my healing journey started. Reiki energy came to stay. I accepted it with an open heart. A smile returned to my face. This smile may differ from before. It has a warmth that can transcend any sadness. It can reach far. Maybe it can reach your heart? Maybe the heart of a dog sitting next to you? The dog who shaped your life, like Rocky shaped mine.

With Ginger following me around, I allowed myself to observe this old soul in a new body that now inhabited my apartment and did everything to make it feel like home. So I created this brief list of similarities and differences between Rocky and Ginger.

What They Have and Don't Have in Common:

Like Rocky, Ginger is a "sniffer" who likes to be in charge. That means if his nose smells a cat, another dog, or any other animal a mile away and you are the lucky one holding his leash, you will run throughout your neighborhood like a lunatic even before you figure out what is going on. Like Rocky, Ginger is a sucker for belly rubs and loves rolling on his back with all four legs up in the air. Like Rocky, Ginger likes to sit by the bathroom door and wait for me to get ready so we can go out. Ginger also has that "will not hurt a fly" Rocky sweetness.

But Ginger fights back when he feels threatened. Still, when he thinks his opponent is stronger, he glues himself to my leg and waits for me to do something about it. Ginger inherited my anxiety about small and crowded places (something that Rocky witnessed on many occasions). He also (proudly) displays that pissy attitude of mine. Both Ginger and I prefer to be in the company of any species but our own. Like Rocky, Ginger doesn't like to share my and Zorel's attention with anyone else. He, too, likes to guard his food and water. Ginger, too, has a husky's high-pitched whine and free-style singing talent. I love when we share crackers, and he crunches and munches them in front of me, occasionally glancing so our eyes can meet. Just like my Rocky. I am amazed at how much his eyes light up with joy when Zorel returns home from school. Then, in Rocky's tap-dancing style, he does what he loves most: he follows her everywhere.

Like Rocky, Ginger is a "delicate flower," having a sensitive stomach when eating food too fast, panting when walking too long, and whining when someone doesn't pay enough attention to him. He is quick to turn away from food that is not "his cup of tea," but if I offer him the same food from my hand, he will eat it. Just like Rocky.

Every day, Ginger uses his body language to prove to me that he is, in fact, Rocky. If you can imagine what a ninety-pound bag of potatoes dropped from a building's second story would sound like, then you know how hard my puppy likes to "hit" the floor when he switches from playing to resting mode. This was one of my favorite things about Rocky. One I missed very much.

When Ginger does that, my inner voice becomes talkative. *C'mon, don't you hear it? That's your baby boy Rocky communicating with you. Now is the best time to focus on opening your senses. Watch. Listen. Love him. Listen again . . . with your heart. Mom, I may not look the same, I may not even act the same. And you knew I would be different. You read enough books and took enough classes to know that we don't carry our physical appearance from one life to another. We might bring some of it with us, the same as we take a part of our heart with us, and part of it is left in Heaven. After all, we are all eighty percent spirit and twenty percent body. The more lives we live, the more spirit we carry with us. Remember, you imagined my soul in a smaller dog's body. Now you have a bigger dog standing before you. But I brought many things with me from my previous life. Those things are unique, and I know how much you loved them. It's me, Mom. Stop questioning. Enjoy every moment of life. Enjoy every moment with me as I do with you. Remember, everything we have is just a moment. Please don't waste it.*

Ginger's excitement when I pick up the leash matches Rocky's. Ginger jumps and hops and jumps some more, and when he does, I can't help but remember Rocky's puppyhood. I do it with a smile now. I embrace every picture from the past that becomes alive before my eyes. Each of them makes my heart dance.

Ginger, unlike Rocky, often marks his territory in a girly style (this is common for puppies, I know). Ginger also does a "boogie dance" (as Zorel calls it) with his doggie bed. I never saw Rocky doing that, probably because he was younger than Ginger when he was neutered. Ginger is still unsure about crowded dog parks and dogs greeting him, but now and then he will find the courage to turn around and sniff them back. That probably has something to do with the little scar he had on his face when we found him. But every time Ginger sees dogs getting in each other's space, he will use Rocky's referee methods to separate them. Like Rocky, Ginger will chase our cat Pumpkin and freeze when our orange tabby turns around and starts hissing.

Ginger likes to pick up any ball and then throw it in the air like a professional basketball player, but like Rocky, he prefers those that squeak so he can squeeze them in his mouth for hours. Like Rocky, nothing is more fun for Ginger than finding a long stick outside, chewing on it for a bit, and then carrying it everywhere. Even better if that stick is in a lake or ocean, and he needs to swim and dive and swim some more to get it. Like Rocky, Ginger will choose swimming over any other outdoor activity, and as soon as his paws get wet, no dog can match his speed and flexibility. Rocky was full of joy and excitement whenever a motorcycle drove past us. His eyes followed it in awe, a smile spreading over his face. Ginger is no different.

Like Rocky, every night Ginger kisses me first and then finds and kisses a spot where he is about to fall asleep. This is the gratitude I am still learning about. And, just like Rocky, Ginger acts as if he has found gold in the grass, but only when it is time to go back home. When Rocky wanted something, he would whine, bark, and repeatedly and loudly yawn just to get my attention. When the situation was urgent, like a potty break, he would sit in front of me and stare at me, then stand up and run in circles, and sit again, and again, and again, and stare, stare, and stare some more.

Ginger, however, takes this to the next level. He yawns so loudly that even the neighbors can hear him. He barks and barks. Then he runs around the room, and if I am lying or sitting down, he jumps on me, licks my face, and stays put until he is convinced I got the point and will get up soon. If I am standing, he stands up and gives me a huge hug that I have difficulty freeing myself from. For Ginger, every situation is urgent. If it is time to play for him, it is time to play for everyone. If he gets hungry in the middle of the night, everyone, including the neighbors, should be up.

Rocky could do something I liked to call "yawning on demand." When I stroked his nose up and down, he would always yawn. Ginger does that too, but his "spot" is closer to his neck than his face. Unlike Rocky, who was always careful not to step on me when coming to bed, Ginger goes straight for my legs and lies on top of them. But Ginger, like Rocky, doesn't stay long in bed or on the carpet. He prefers sleeping on the floor. Somewhere between Zorel's and my bedroom door is his favorite sleeping place. It is as if he tries to show me every day that, with him, there is no single thing I will ever forget about Rocky.

Anyone who witnessed Rocky's rolling-in-grass performance could tell how much he enjoyed it. People would smile while passing by, calling him a "happy dog." Ginger loves rolling in the grass, but unlike Rocky, he will also roll in the mud. People will smile and laugh, calling him a "mudskipper."

Ginger's behavior also shows me that a soul takes its old fears, likes, and dislikes into its new life. In Rocky's golden years, our smoke alarm went off a few times while I was baking something. Since then, he wouldn't let me out of his sight whenever I was in the kitchen, and every time I would reach for the oven, he would run away and hide. Ginger is like that, always in the other room, waiting for me to finish cooking. Rocky's ears would instantly fall past his face when he saw a hairbrush in my hand. Ginger does the same. Slices of cheese were Rocky's favorite treat and one of the only foods he could eat in his last days. Ginger would turn down the juiciest steak for any type of cheese.

Ginger is still uncomfortable in the car like Rocky was during our first rides. But as soon as I rolled the window down, Rocky put his head out, started flapping his ears, and never looked back. Ginger follows suit. One month prior to his transition, Rocky's ears were often up, and more pointy, as if he wanted to show me how he would look in his next life.

Ginger's ears are pointy. I like the way he tilts his head when he listens to me. He is learning fast. He is also teaching me about life, people, and myself. And more than anything else, he is trying to show me what patience is all about. He has to. We still have many lessons to learn—together. Isn't that one of the main reasons for his return? I am ready. But deep in my heart, I feel that this time he is here to focus on another human: my daughter. She needs someone by her side besides me. Her words contain simplicity, wisdom, and pure child emotions. "Rocky makes everything better."

Ginger's fur has three colors like Rocky's, and his signature is a black spot on his right shoulder that resembles a tiny bottle cap. Many years ago, when I worked in grooming, I used to take Rocky to work every day. There, I often pampered him with special baths and different hairstyles. Rocky's fur grew fast, and between each haircut, a little, black circle-shaped mark appeared close to his shoulder. Sometimes there was one, and sometimes there were two.

Ginger, like Rocky, does something I like to call "tongue dancing." While he sleeps, I often hear him munching through the air. He also often shows me something I miss about Rocky, especially when I need quiet time. When I see him jumping in the air to catch a little fly, I remember that with Rocky around, that perfectly annoying buzzing sound never lasted too long.

But nobody showed me more clearly that Ginger is Rocky than another dog. Her name is Lily. Lily is one of Ginger's favorite friends. They are so close that I often joke Lily is his girlfriend. There's nothing unusual about all of this. Right? But the other day, my phone showed me a photo memory from four years ago when I lived in Houston. Rocky rests his head on another dog's shoulder in this particular photo. I remember this dog very well, and I often called her Rocky's girlfriend. She was a standard gray poodle, just like Lily from San Antonio. She loved playing with Rocky, and they always had so much fun. And I remember very clearly that her name was Lily too. When I showed the photo to Lily's human, she glanced at our dogs and then looked at me with a "did you just take that picture" expression on her face.

Every time we have come across people Rocky knew well, Ginger runs to give them his big-doggie hugs, and he, differently from Rocky, is not a very stranger-trusting dog. He wags his tail when they (accidentally) call him "Rocky." Then he runs back to me and stretches his long face in a smile when I say, "Wolfie, let's go home."

This is how the universe connected all the dots and created the complete picture—an exquisite picture I wake up every morning feeling thankful for, always in awe of having it in my life.

About three weeks after my daughter and I moved to San Antonio, we visited a majestic place called the Japanese Tea Garden. In this garden, we came across a man walking a German shepherd. Of course, Zorel wanted to pet the dog because he reminded her of Rocky. I did too. His human companion and I started up a conversation. He told me about South Side Lions Park. Three weeks later, Zorel and I went there. About two weeks after our first visit to the park, we found Ginger nearby.

Rocky saved my life twice. First by giving up on this world for me and the second time by giving up on Heaven so we could be together again. I am happy we still share a small space in this big world. But some things make me sad and a bit worried. Many old experiences are coming back to life. Like everything is repeating itself.

Ginger is a high-energy puppy who sometimes makes me impatient. Then there are those similar to nursing and diaper-changing responsibilities that come with a puppy. He is hungry. He needs to go out. He has diarrhea. He gets into the trash. He throws up. He eats grass. Throws up again. He marks our neighbor's car wheels. He jumps. He chews on walls, furniture, important papers, shoes, and clothes. He needs to play. He needs to run. He needs to put his head in my lap. He needs to put his paws across the pages of my book. He needs to chew the squeaker inside his toy ten thousand times. He takes a short nap and then goes back to chewing. He needs to keep an eye on me even when he sleeps. Anything and everything. *Do I really want to deal with all this? Am I ready for an attachment like this? Do I want such a commitment?* Then I look into his eyes and remember I had the same thought thirteen years ago when he was a puppy in another life.

I also remember the love that I have in my heart for Rocky. The effort I am making is so tiny compared to his efforts to come back to me. And every time, I feel crazy—because I know that's what people will think of me if I tell them what's happening in my life right now—I look at Ginger lying next to the door instead of in his bed. Check. Rocky's old habit. Then I take him for a walk, and someone calls him a wolf. Check. People called Rocky the same. Ginger gets ready for bed by scratching the floor, turning around, and scratching the floor some more. Then he decides to call it a night somewhere else. Check. Rocky always made me smile by doing the same thing. Ginger sits beside me and waits for my hand to caress his fur. Check. I always loved when Rocky did that.

I post Ginger's picture on Rocky's internet pages, and people think Rocky is ready for another adventure. This is not a dream. I just saw my reflection in the mirror. My eyes are open. This can't be more real. Check. I asked Rocky for a stray dog and hoped that would be him when the one crossed my path. And he responded. One stray dog led me to the next, and the next, and the next one. Until the one I was waiting for came to me.

I knew he would be different in some ways. What I didn't realize was that I would be able to count those differences on one hand.

I often have to keep closing my eyes and opening them again to ensure I am not watching a movie that will end soon. This is real life, and I can't stop thanking all the gods and angels. I can't stop replacing worries with smiles. Rocky wanted me to survive the biggest loss in my life, start believing in myself, and know that nothing is impossible when you let love take the lead. My love led me to find him again. His love led him to forever adopt a child and a woman nobody else wanted. Our rock. Our star. Our Rocky.

So many times, I asked myself, *Why did I receive all those messages from Rocky in spirit if he was already on Earth, getting ready to be born? Or was Rocky's soul looking for a young, healthy body on Earth and at the same time communicating with me from Heaven?* In my ongoing research on the afterlife, I learned that the living sometimes contracts with those in spirit to trade places. This is called a "walk in." It usually happens when one on Earth has a hard life and is ready to give up on it. Ginger lived as a stray in San Antonio, and like many other city street dogs, he was depressed and defeated.

I still wasn't sure. I kept asking my spirit guides and my angel guardians for the answer. Then one night I was awakened by a touch on my hand. I opened my eyes but soon closed them again. I kept them shut out of fear as I felt someone trying to pull my hand toward them. I was aware that it wasn't a living being but a spirit's energy. I didn't know whose energy it was. "It's Rocky. It's Rocky." I heard the words in my mind. I still didn't feel Rocky's soul there. I still felt weird.

Months later, after pushing that dream out of my mind, I sat down to do my daily meditation. Soon I felt my grandmother's energy around me. I was happy. I told her how much I loved and missed her. I asked her to visit me in my dreams. She did that very same night.

In my dream, my grandmother was lying next to me. Her head was resting close to mine, like in good old times. She seemed much healthier and happier than in the last year of her life. We didn't talk much. We just enjoyed being together again.

I tried to stay in the dream as long as possible, but I couldn't stay as long as I wanted. I woke up feeling peace and joy. I also woke up thinking of things I loved so much about my Baba. Some of her habits were simple and lovable, like those of a small child. One of them was to pull my hand closer to her when she had something important to tell me. Then something occurred to me. Her spirit visited me that night when I was sleeping; it was her energy that touched my hand and started pulling it, and her beautiful soul telling me "It's Rocky. It's Rocky." All that while Ginger was in the next room, squeezing the squeaky toy in his mouth and waiting for me to take him out. I got my answer. I knew that I was embraced by eternal truth coming from my spirit guide, from the spiritual dimensions. This touch forever changed my three-dimensional limited beliefs and expectations.

It could be that many of my requests to connect to Rocky in the spirit world were answered by my grandmother. It could be that once the soul and spirit leave the physical body, the other side becomes the spirit's forever home, but the soul can still travel to Earth and start a new life around its "old" people. I will probably find out when I go to the light myself. But now I am sure my grandmother knows my dog and I have reunited in this life again. She knew that he was waiting to be born again in 2021. The same as she knew that my daughter was waiting to be born in 2014. Now I know the rainbow my daughter and I saw on October 16 (one of the first days we took Ginger to the dog park) was a sign from my grandmother. My grandmother: the only human who helped me grow up with the hope for goodness on Earth—humanity, compassion, and dignity. And the only human who helped me grow spiritually and believe in divinity.

Now I know that as multidimensional human beings, we can choose to connect with a multidimensional universe or stay attached to the three-dimensional world around us. If we don't see something, it doesn't mean it is not there to guide us, love us, and give our life meaning. After all, the air is a source of life, but we can't see it. We watch television but don't see electromagnetic waves that make it possible for us to see the pictures. We send love to someone, but we don't see the shape of it; we only know the difference it makes in their life. Every day, I see the difference love makes in my life. Every day, I know what Aristotle meant by *entelechy*—potential energy (formless) becomes actual energy (matter). Love brings us back to life. Over and over again.

Love also reminds us that life is happening right now. Months after having Ginger by my side, I caught myself browsing through old pictures on my phone more often than noticing his adorable belly screaming for my rubs. Not long after that, my phone froze, and I lost thousands of photos in my attempt to fix it. But my puppy was still by my side, wagging his tail and touching my hand with his paw.

Dear Rocky,

I am thinking of you. Now. Every day. Forever. You taught me so much about my soul in the past fifteen months. Because of you, I know that what is in my heart and mind will never cease to exist. Never.

Today I am donating the supplements I bought for you, hoping they would heal you. Many of them are still unopened. I am sending them to strangers with whom I have something in common. They are people who fight cancer to save the lives of their fur babies. They fight hard. This may help them win. I wish for that.

Today I am also donating your book, Rocky and a Girl with a Curl, to a non-profit organization called Hindi's Libraries. Hindi's Libraries was created to keep the memory of Dr. Hindi Krinsky alive. She died in 2018 at the age of thirty-two. Their current campaign, Pages for Paws, is very close to my heart because it supports children, pets, and a love for reading. Loving animals and reading books can help humans to become better people. And for someone like me, this can help to survive.

If I am to die tomorrow, you and Zorel, my Rocky and my girl with a curl, you are my legacy. There is also this book I am still working on. There are other books as well. If this is my last day, what are the last words I want to say? And here, Rocky, I am telling them to you.

First, I would say: Thank you, God, for Ginger. After spending a few months with him, I do not doubt that you, Rocky, came back to me. He does everything you did. Staying close to Mama in case other dogs want to fight but standing between his sister and any dog regardless of its size and strength. Snuggling. Giving cute, begging looks. Barking endlessly when it is time to go out. Giving the precious gift of love.

Second, always protect your sister like that. Don't let anyone, including relatives, hurt her. None of her "family on paper" would love and care for her. Protect her as best as you can.

Third, my soul and my heart will never be far from the two of you. You, Rocky, know that very well, and Zorel is going to learn. Nothing but love lives forever. And Heaven is never far from the Earth when love connects them.

Last but not least, wherever I am, I want to keep donating my books to good causes like Hindi's Libraries. The world needs to know about the two of you; the world needs stories like yours. The world needs more untraditional families that will be embraced and rescued by the compassionate, loving heart of a dog. The world needs more love.

A study was published in 2015 entitled *Ten Days of Darkness Causes Temporary Blindness During an Early Critical Period in Feline*. It showed that when five-week-old kittens spend ten days in darkness, they emerge blind. It can take up to seven weeks for them to recover and see again.

There is a reason I was exposed to the darkness of the world at a very young age. It took years, decades, for me to see the light again. Whatever that reason is, I am grateful for it because it brought Rocky into my life.

November 10, 2021

I never knew that one year could feel like a century when you grieve. I am sitting in my room and remembering how it felt to watch Rocky's body becoming still. Everything comes back again. All the memories. All the tears. The fact that Ginger is here doesn't make me miss Rocky any less. His ears flapped so adorably when he walked, the ears that I loved to kiss so much. His eyes were blue and brown, eyes that followed me everywhere. The softness of his fur called for my embrace.

When people said to me, "Pain of losing a pet doesn't go away," I found these words to be so depressing and scary. But now I know what they meant. I now understand that we grieve as long as we live. How can one not grieve a loss of such a beautiful soul in a world full of souls turning away from, denying, any beauty? Yes, we grieve as long as we live. That's okay. That's fine. We love them as long as we live. They love us in life and beyond it. I open the door and walk into the living room. I know Ginger is waiting for me there. I want to hug him. I want to enjoy every moment as Rocky taught me. I want to enjoy it as if it were my first and my last. I dance through life. I am grateful for it. I finally understand that not everyone is blessed in the same way. I am thankful for my blessings. I am thankful for Rocky's love.

ROCKY

On the morning of March 9, 2024, we found a cat lying near our doorstep.

It is common for our neighbors to leave their pets outside sometimes; the cat would be back home when we returned—or so I thought. My daughter went inside the apartment to bring some treats. She had a hard time taking her eyes and hands off a beautiful white and gray tabby.

"We have to go," I had to remind her a few times before she followed me to our car.

Four hours later the cat was still in the same spot waiting for us. So I knelt next to her and scooped her into my arms. We drove to a pet clinic where they scanned her for a microchip. As I assumed, she belonged to someone but whoever that someone was, they never answered their phone or called me back.

We named her Coco. She was gentle. She was special. She was very comfortable around us. Especially around a pushy Ginger's nose getting in her face and sniffing her whiskers.

On day six, I noticed that Coco's breathing changed from peaceful to labor. That lasted only for a few minutes and she was back to normal. But my inner voice kept repeating heart, heart.

Two days later, in the emergency room, we found that Coco's heart was enlarged and together with her lungs drowning in fluid.

Like Rocky, she was put on oxygen. Like Rocky, she waited for me to put my arms around her and say everything will be okay. Like Rocky, she needed me to pull the plug on her suffering. But unlike with Rocky, I didn't back away from making a decision. I decided to let her go. In peace.

On March 16, 2024, I held her and she placed her little head in my hand. I told her that seven days were more than enough for me to love her with all my heart. I told her how perfect she was.

On March 16, 2024, I proved to my boy that now I know letting go has nothing to do with giving up. That dying is not the end. That heart can stop but love will continue to live.

While holding Coco in my arms, kissing her, and telling her how much she meant to me, I cried for both Rocky and her. I called their names while embracing their journeys to captivating eternity. I embraced their journey back to me—Ginger and . . . whatever I would call Coco the next time I see her. Because with angels like them, everything is extraordinary. Everything is possible.

First picture of Ginger

ROCKY

Halloween 2019—with Rocky

Halloween 2023—with Ginger

Christmas 2018—with Rocky

Christmas 2023—with Ginger

ROCKY

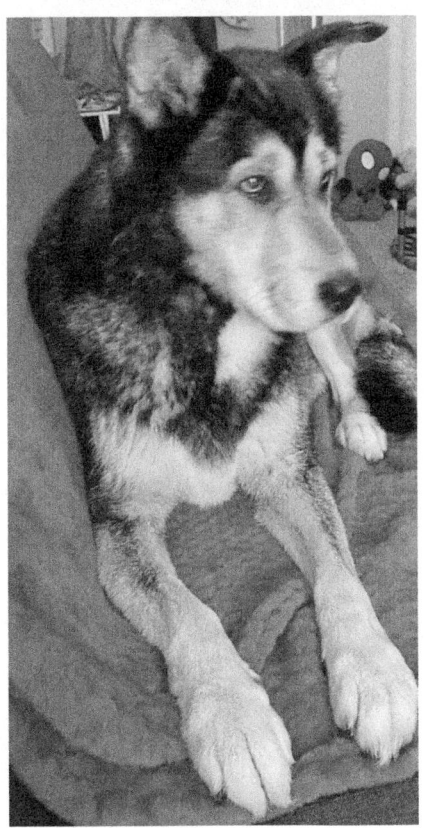

ROCKY

SNJEZANA MARINKOVIC

ROCKY

AUTHOR'S NOTE

Dear reader, here are some pages you may like to follow to join me in spreading the word about abandoned, afraid, and lost animals.

Dogs Teach Love
https://www.instagram.com/dogsteachlove

Rocky and a Girl With a Curl
https://www.facebook.com/rockyandagirlwithacurl

Urgent Death Row Dogs and Cats
https://www.facebook.com/share/fdeDTKLqg7vfK63c

Dogvengers Assemble
https://www.facebook.com/share/8kDSGNAXV77hgs8q

Stolen and Missing Pets of Texas
https://www.facebook.com/share/68RGTCk31j2Rvpbk

AUTHOR'S NOTE

Spotting Spot-Lost Pets of Texas
https://www.facebook.com/share/4Thh5fMcPPdPHp3u

Dead Dog Walking Legacy
https://www.facebook.com/share/YvkrknjG3jxc6ahd

I often sit next to my pets, including those that I take in from the streets or foster from animal shelters, and read books. This is what truly makes me peaceful and happy. If you enjoy doing the same, "We Love Memoirs" provides some great book recommendations:
https://www.facebook.com/share/LfUvsLa42ZEgukp8

Thank you for allowing me to share Rocky's story with you. If you know anyone who suffers from pet loss, please share it with them. Books helped me with my grief and my book may help someone with theirs. Let the energy of love reach many hearts.

Made in the USA
Middletown, DE
09 April 2025

74054545R00136